Corner House Publishers

SOCIAL SCIENCE REPRINTS

General Editor MAURICE FILLER

THE

DIARY

OF

GEORGE WASHINGTON,

FROM 1789 TO 1791;

EMBRACING

THE OPENING OF THE FIRST CONGRESS,

AND

HIS TOURS THROUGH NEW ENGLAND, LONG ISLAND,
AND THE SOUTHERN STATES.

TOGETHER WITH

HIS JOURNAL OF A TOUR TO THE OHIO,
IN 1753.

EDITED BY BENSON J. LOSSING.

CORNER HOUSE PUBLISHERS

WILLIAMSTOWN, MASSACHUSETTS 01267

1978

REPRINTED 1978

BY

CORNER HOUSE PUBLISHERS

Printed in the United States of America

INTRODUCTORY REMARKS.

It has been truthfully said that posterity loves details. When we contemplate the men who have lived before us, and left impressions of their acts upon the social aspect of the generation in which they moved, we feel a great desire to become acquainted with the details of their daily lives,—how they spent their time not devoted to those public duties which have given them a title to a place in history, what were their recreations in times of leisure, and who were their family associates and their chosen companions in private. Historic men really form a part of our own being, for the man of to-day is only the more complete man of a thousand years ago, made so by the intervening experiences. In this unity, felt, even though not comprehended by us all, doubtless lies the secret spring of our yearnings for knowledge respecting the past life of the race which render History and Biography specially attractive.

Of all the records of men's doings, none possess so lively an interest, because so evidently truthful, as DIARIES—the current history of the common every-day life of the men who made the chronicles of moving events, even while the majestic procession of the hours was passing by. In these, Posterity finds those details it so much loves. The general historian must necessarily omit many of them; and the biographer too often leaves them unnoticed while unfolding to view the public acts of his subject. And so the world loses the best elements of history, by which one age may judge philosophically of the character of another, as revealed by the knowledge of their common life.

There is a continual and rapidly growing desire in the hearts of Americans to know more and more of the life and character of Washington, in all its minute details. We listen with the most eager attention to the words of revered men (now so few) who have seen the FATHER OF HIS COUNTRY; and the memory receives these narratives so perfectly, that, amid the thousand other impressions, they are never effaced. Fortunately for posterity, Washington was eminently a man of method. He was careful about small things as well as great; and it was his custom, from early years, to make a record of the events of his daily life, for future reference. This habit he continued until the close of his life; and these notes, kept in books of convenient size for carrying in the pocket, furnish some of the most interesting pictures of the habits and modes of thinking of the beloved Hero and Sage, that have come down to us. Many of them have disappeared, and are doubtless lost forever. Like the Sibylline leaves, they are becoming more precious as their numbers decrease; and we ought to take special care that the contents of those that remain shall not be lost. To do this, the agency of the printing-press must be evoked in multiplying copies, in numbers sufficient to guarantee the preservation of the precious words.

The Diaries printed in the following pages, constitute some of the most important of Washington's private records, being made while he and his compatriots were arranging and putting in motion the machinery of our federal government. They are comprised in two little volumes, numbered respectively, 13, and 14. They are oblong in form, about four inches in width, and six inches in length, and contain from sixty to eighty leaves.

All of Washington's earlier diaries were kept on the blank

leaves of the *Virginia Almanac*, "Printed and sold by Purdie and Dixon, Williamsburg." Later ones were kept in other pocket almanacs. The greater portion of his diaries are in the office of the rolls, State Department, Washington City. Those printed in this volume, are in private hands. A few illustrative and explanatory notes have been inserted to render some observations clearer to the reader.

B. J. L.

New York, July, 1860.

DIARY

FROM

THE 1st DAY OF OCTOBER, 1789,

UNTIL

THE 1st OF JUNE, 1791.

OCTOBER, 1789.

Thursday, 1st.

Exercised in my carriage in the forenoon.

The following company dined here to-day, viz:

Mr. Read, of the Senate, Col⁰· Bland and Mr. Madison, of the House of Representatives, Mr. Osgood and his lady, Col⁰· Duer, his lady and Miss Brown, Col⁰· Lewis Morris and lady, lady Christiana Griffin and her daughter, and Judge Duane and Mrs. Greene.[1]

Mr. Thomas Nelson joined my family this day.

Dispatched many of the Com'ns for the Judiciary Judges, Marshalls, and Attorneys this day, with the Acts.

Friday, 2d.

Dispatching Commissions, &c., as yesterday, for the Judiciary.

The visitors to Mrs. Washington this evening were not numerous.

Saturday, 3d.

Sat for Mr. Rammage near two hours to-day, who was drawing a miniature Picture of me for Mrs. Washington.[2]

Walked in the afternoon, and sat about two o'clock for Madam de Brehan, to complete a miniature profile of me,

---

1 The widow of General Nathaniel Greene.

2 John Rammage was a native of Ireland. He married a lady in

which she had begun from memory, and which she had made exceedingly like the original.[3]

SUNDAY, 4th.

Went to St. Paul's Chappel[4] in the forenoon. Spent the remainder of the day in writing private letters for to-morrow's Post.

MONDAY, 5th.

Dispatched the Commissions to all the Judges of the Supreme and District Courts; and to the Marshalls and Attorneys—and accompanied them with all the Acts respecting the Judiciary Department.

Exercised on horseback between the hours of 9 and 11 in the forenoon, and between 5 and 6 in the afternoon, on foot.

Boston, and went to Halifax with the British troops in the spring of 1776. Early in 1777, he established himself as a miniature painter, in William-street, New York, where he "continued to paint all the military heroes or beaux of the garrison, and all the belles of the place," says Dunlap. For many years after the war, he continued to be the best miniature-painter in New York, and occasionally made crayon or pastil sketches of life size. He died soon after painting the miniature of Washington.

[3] This was the Marchioness de Brehan (or Brienne), sister of the Count de Moustier, Minister from France, who, with her son, accompanied her brother to this country. They all visited Mount Vernon in the autumn of 1788. The "miniature in profile" of the first President which she made in New York, was engraved in Paris, and several impressions of it were sent to Washington the following summer. See Count de Moustier's letter to Washington, May 11, 1790, and Washington's letter to the Count, November 1, 1790, in Sparks' *Life and Writings of Washington*.

[4] Washington's pew in St. Paul's chapel was on the north side, under the gallery, about half way between the chancel and the vestry room.

Had conversation with Col⁰· Hamilton on the propriety of my making a tour through the Eastern States during the recess of Congress, to acquire knowledge of the face of the Country, the growth and agriculture thereof—and the temper and disposition of the inhabitants towards the new government, who thought it a very desirable plan, and advised it accordingly.

TUESDAY, 6th.

Exercised in a carriage with Mrs. Washington in the forenoon.

Conversed with Gen. Knox, Secretary at War, on the above tour, who also recommended it accordingly.

Signed Letters of Instructions to the Governor of the Western Territory respecting the situation of matters in that quarter. And authorized him, in case the hostile disposition of the Indians was such as to make it necessary to call out the Militia, and time would not allow him to give me previous notice of it, to apply to the States of Virginia and Pennsylvania for a number not exceeding 1,500; one thousand of which to be taken from the former, and five hundred from the latter.

WEDNESDAY, 7th.

Exercised on horseback, and called on the Vice-President. In the afternoon walked an hour.

Mr. Jay communicated the purpt. of the Instructions received by Sir John Temple, British Consul, from the Duke of Leeds, Secretary for Foreign Affairs, viz:

Trade. How many *foreign* vessels—of what nations—whether from Europe or their Colonies.

What tonnage—whether any and what difference between *British* and others—what on *American.*

What *Port charges* on foreign vessels—whether any and what difference, &c.

What *duties* on foreign goods—whether any and what difference as to the *Countries* producing, and *vessels* bringing them—number of vessels *built*, where, &c.

Staple Commodities.—Whether they encrease or diminish—which—in what degree—and why.

Manufactures—what—where—whether and how encouraged.

Emigrations — From *Europe*, in what numbers—from where—whether and how encouraged, &c.—from *United States*—to British and Spanish territories, &c.

Population—whether generally, or partially encreasing, or diminishing, and from what causes.

Justice—Whether there be any, and what obstructions, and where, to the recovery of British Debts according to treaty.

Upon consulting Mr. Jay on the propriety of my intended tour into the Eastern States, he highly approved of it, but observed, a similar visit w'd be expected by those of the Southern.[5]

With the same gentleman I had conversation on the pro-

---

[5] Washington visited the Southern States in the spring of 1791. He set out from Mount Vernon early in April, and was gone three months, during which time he performed a journey of about nineteen hundred miles, with the same span of horses. He followed the seaboard to Savannah, visited Augusta, and returned by way of the interior of the Carolinas and Virginia.

priety of tak'g informal means of ascertaining the views of the British Court with respect to our Western Posts in their possession, and to a Commercial treaty. He thought steps of this sort advisable, and mentioned as a fit person for this purpose, a Doctr. Bancroft,[6] as a man in whom entire confidence might be placed.

Col[o.] Hamilton on the same subject highly approved of the measure, but thought Mr. Gouv'r. Morris well qualified.

Thursday, 8th.

Mr. Gardoqui[7] took leave, proposing to embark to-morrow for Spain.

The following company dined with me to-day, viz:

The Vice-President, his lady and son and her niece, with their son-in-law, Col[o.] Smith and his lady—Governor Clinton and his two eldest daughters—Mr. Dalton and his lady, their son-in-law, Mr. Dubois, and his lady, and their other three daughters.

In the evening, the Count de Moustier and Madam de Brehan came in and sat an hour.

Mr. Madison took his leave to-day. He saw no impro-

---

[6] Edward Bancroft, M. D., was an American by birth, but settled as a physician in London. He was intimate with Dr. Franklin, and a friend to the American cause during the war for Independence. He was with Silas Deane, in Paris, for some time; and in the diplomatic operations of the United States, during the war, he was an efficient auxiliary. Dr. Bancroft was a Fellow of the Royal Society of London, and gained much repute as author of "An Essay on the Natural History of Guiana," and "Experimental Researches concerning the Philosophy of Permanent Colors."

[7] Spanish diplomatic agent, who came to the United States in 1785.

priety in my trip to the eastward; but with respect to the private agent to ascertain the disposition of the British Court with respect to the Western Posts and a Commercial treaty, he thought if the necessity did not press, it would be better to wait the arrival of Mr. Jefferson, who might be able to give the information wanted on this head—and with me thought that if Mr. Gouv'r. Morris was employed in this business, it would be a commitment for his appointment as Minister, if one should be sent to that Court, or wanted at Versailles in place of Mr. Jefferson, and moreover if either of these was his wish, whether his representations might not be made with an eye to it. He thought with Col⁰· Hamilton, and as Mr. Jay also does, that Mr. Morris is a man of superior talents—but with the latter that his imagination sometimes runs ahead of his judgment—that his manners before he is known, and where known, had created opinions of himself that were not favourable to him, and which he did not merit.[8]

FRIDAY, 9th.

Exercised on horseback between the hours of 9 and 11. Visited in my route the gardens of Mr. Perry and Mr. Williamson.[9]

---

[8] Mr. Morris was then in France, but not in any official capacity. He was intrusted with the business alluded to, and Washington prepared the necessary credentials for him on the 13th of October.

[9] Perry's garden was on the west side of the Bloomingdale road, west of the present Union Square, and occupied the ground whereon the Church of the Puritans and other edifices now stand. Williamson's was a flower and nursery garden, and a place of public resort, on the

Received from the French Minister, in person, official notice of his having recd. leave to return to his Court, and intended embarkation—and the orders of his Court to make the following communication, viz :

That his Majesty was pleased at the alteration which had taken place in our Government, and congratulated this Country on the choice they had made of a Presid't.

He added that *he* should take care to make a favourable representation of the present state of things here to his Master, who, he doubted not, would be much pleased therewith. Hitherto he observed that the Government of this Country had been of so fluctuating a nature, no dependence could be placed on its proceedings; wh'h caused foreign nations to be cautious of entering into Treaties, &c., with the United States. But under the present Government there is a head to look up to—and power being put into the hands of its officers, stability will be derived from its doings.

The visiters this evening to Mrs. Washington were respectable, both of gentlemen and ladies.

Saturday, 10th.

Pursuant to an engagement formed on Thursday last, I set off about 9 o'clock in my barge to visit Mr. Prince's fruit gardens and shrubberies at Flushing, on Long Island. The Vice-President, Governor of the State, Mr. Izard, Col°· Smith, and Majr. Jackson accompanied me.

---

east side of Greenwich-street, extending about three squares up from Harrison-street.

These gardens, except in the number of young fruit trees, did not answer my expectations. The shrubs were trifling, and the flowers not numerous.

The inhabitants of this place shewed us what respect they could, by making the best use of one cannon to salute.

On our return we stopped at the seats of General and Mr. Gouvernr. Morris, and viewed a barn, of which I have heard the latter speak much, belonging to his farm—but it was not of a construction to strike my fancy—nor did the conveniences of it at all answer their cost. From hence we proceeded to Harlaem, where we were met by Mrs. Washington, Mrs. Adams and Mrs. Smith. Dined at the tavern kept by a Capt. Mariner,[10] and came home in the evening.

SUNDAY, 11th.

At home all day—writing private letters.

MONDAY, 12th.

Received the compliments of the Count de Penthere, commanding his most Christian Majesty's Squadron in the harbour of Boston—these were sent by the Marquis de Tra-versy in the Active Frigate; who, with all his officers were presented by the French Minister at one o'clock.

---

[10] Captain Marriner was an eccentric character, and was associated with Captain Hyler in whale-boat warfare in the vicinity of New York, during a part of the Revolution. On one occasion he was concerned in an attempt to capture Mayor Mathews and other violent Tories, who resided at Flatbush, near Brooklyn. Marriner lived at Harlem and on Ward's Island, for many years after the war, and kept a tavern at each place.

Tuesday, 13th.

At two o'clock received the Address from the People called Quakers.

A good many gentlemen attended the Levee this day.

Wednesday, 14th.

Wrote several letters to France, and about 7 o'clock in the afternoon made an informal visit with Mrs. Washington to the Count de Moustier and Madame de Brehan, to take leave of them. Into the hands of the former I committed these letters, viz: to the Count de Estaing, Count de Rochambeau, the Marqs. de la Fayette and the Marqs. de la Rouirie.

Having resolved to write to Mr. Gouvr. Morris, to request as a private agent that he wd. sound the intention of the British Ministry with respect to their fulfilment of the Treaty—and dispositions towards a Commercial Treaty with us, the letters were prepared and lodged in the hands of Mr. Jay to forward.

Thursday, 15th.

Commenced my Journey about 9 o'clock for Boston and a tour through the Eastern States.

The Chief Justice, Mr. Jay—and the Secretaries of the Treasury and War Departments accompanied me some distance out of the city. About 10 o'clock it began to Rain, and continued to do so till 11, when we arrived at the house of one Hoyatt, who keeps a Tavern at Kings-bridge, where we, that is, Major Jackson, Mr. Lear and myself, with six servants, which composed my Retinue, dined.

After dinner, through frequent light showers we proceed'd to the Tavern of a Mrs. Haviland at Rye; who keeps a very neat and decent Inn.

The Road for the greater part, indeed the whole way, was very rough and stoney, but the Land strong, well covered with grass and a luxuriant crop of Indian Corn intermixed with Pompions (which were yet ungathered) in the fields. We met four droves of Beef Cattle for the New York Market, (about 30 in a drove) some of which were very fine—also a flock of Sheep for the same place. We scarcely passed a farm house that did not abd. in Geese.

Their Cattle seemed to be of a good quality, and their hogs large, but rather long legged. No dwelling house is seen without a Stone or Brick Chimney, and rarely any without a shingled roof—*generally* the sides are of shingles also.

The distance of this day's travel was 31 miles, in which we passed through (after leaving the Bridge) East Chester, New Rochelle, and Mamaroneck; but as these places (though they have houses of worship in them) are not regularly laid out, they are scarcely to be distinguished from the intermediate farms, which are very close together—and separated, as one Inclosure from another also is, by fences of stone, which are indeed easily made, as the country is immensely stoney. Upon enquiry we find their crops of Wheat and Rye have been abundant—though of the first they had sown rather sparingly on acct. of the destruction which had of late years been made of that grain by what is called the Hessian fly.[11]

---

[11] A small two-winged fly or midge, which has long been very destructive to young wheat in the United States. It has now almost dis-

FRIDAY, 16th.

About 7 o'clock we left the Widow Haviland's, and after passing Horse Neck, six miles distant from Rye, the Road through which is hilly and immensely stoney, and trying to Wheels and Carriages, we breakfasted at Stamford, which is 6 miles further, (at one Webb's,) a tolerable good house, but not equal in appearance or reality to Mrs. Haviland's. In this Town are an Episcopal Church and a meeting house. At Norwalk, which is ten miles further, we made a halt to feed our Horses. To the lower end of this town Sea Vessels come, and at the other end are Mills, Stores, and an Episcopal and Presbiterian Church.

From hence to Fairfield, where we dined and lodged, is 12 miles; and part of it very rough Road, but not equal to that thro' Horse Neck. The superb Landscape, however, which is to be seen from the meeting house of the latter is a rich regalia. We found all the Farmers busily employed in gathering, grinding, and expressing the Juice of their apples; the crop of which they say is rather above mediocrity. The average crop of Wheat they add, is about 15 bushels to the acre from their fallow land—often 20, and from that to 25. The Destructive evidences of British cruelty are yet visible both in Norwalk and Fairfield; as there are the chimneys of many burnt houses standing in them yet.[12] The principal export from Norwalk and Fair-

---

appeared. It was a common opinion that it was brought from Europe by the *Hessians*, as the German troops were called, who came over in the pay of Great Britain, in 1776.

[12] These, with Danbury, were desolated by a force of British, Hessians, and Tories, under Governor Tryon, in 1777.

field is Horses and Cattle—salted Beef and Pork—Lumber
and Indian Corn, to the West Indies, and in a small degree
Wheat and Flour.

SATURDAY, 17th.

A little after sun-rise we left Fairfield, and passing
through Et. Fairfield breakfasted at Stratford, wch. is ten
miles from Fairfield, and is a pretty village on or near Stratford Rivr. The Road between these two places is not on
the whole bad (for this country)—in some places very gd.,
especially through Et. Fairfield, wch. is in a plain, and free
from stone.

There are two decent looking Churches in this place,
though small, viz: an Episcopal, and Presbyterian or Con-
gregationalist (as they call themselves). At Stratford there
is the same. At this place I was received with an effort
of Military parade; and was attended to the Ferry, which
is near a mile from the center of the Town, by sevl. Gentlemen on horseback. Doctr. Johnson[13] of the Senate, visited me here, being with Mrs. Johnson in this Town,
(where he formerly resided). The Ferry is near half a
mile; and sometimes much incommoded by winds and
cross tides. The navigation for vessels of about 75 Tons
extends up to Danby, ten miles higher, where it is said
there is a pretty brisk trade. At Stratford they are estab-

---

[13] William Samuel Johnson, LL. D., who was a member of the "Stamp
Act Congress," held at New York, in 1765, and was active in public
life for about forty years. He was a member of the convention that
framed the Federal Constitution; was the first Senator from Connecticut in the new Congress; and was President of Columbia College from
1792 until 1800.

lishing a manufactory of Duck, and have lately turned out about 400 bolts. From the Ferry it is abt. 3 miles to Milford, which is situated in more uneven and stony grd. than the 3 last villages through wch. we passed. In this place there is but one Church, or in other words, but one steeple—but there are Grist and Saw mills, and a handsome Cascade over the Tumbling dam; but one of the prettiest things of this kind is at Stamford, occasioned also by damming the water for their mills; it is near 100 yds. in width, and the water now being of a proper height, and the rays of the sun striking upon it as we passed, had a pretty effect upon the foaming water as it fell. From Milford we took the lower road through West haven, part of which was good and part rough, and arrived at New Haven before two o'clock; we had time to walk through several parts of the City before Dinner. By taking the lower Road we missed a Committee of the Assembly, who had been appointed to wait upon and escort me into town—to prepare an address —and to conduct me when I should leave the City as far as they should judge proper. The address was presented at 7 o'clock—and at nine I received another address from the Congregational Clergy of the place. Between the rect. of the two addresses I received the Compliment of a visit from the Govr. Mr. Huntington — the Lieut. Govr. Mr. Wolcott—and the Mayor, Mr. Roger Sherman.

The City of New-haven occupies a good deal of ground, but is thinly, though regularly laid out and built. The number of Souls in it are said to be about 4000. There is an Episcopal Church and 3 Congregational Meeting Houses and a College, in which there are at this time about 120

Students under auspices of Doctr. Styles. The Harbour of this place is not good for large vessels—abt. 16 belong to it. The Linnen manufacture does not appear to be of so much importance as I had been led to believe. In a word, I could hear but little of it. The Exports from this City are much the same as from Fairfield, &c., and flax seed, (chiefly to New York). The Road from Kingsbridge to this place runs as near the Sound as the Bays and Inlets will allow, but from hence to Hartford it leaves the Sound and runs more to the Northward.

SUNDAY, 18th.

Went in the forenoon to the Episcopal Church, and in the afternoon to one of the Congregational Meeting-Houses. Attended to the first by the Speaker of the Assembly, Mr. Edwards, and a Mr. Ingersoll, and to the latter by the Governor, the Lieut. Governor, the Mayor, and Speaker.

These Gentlemen all dined with me, (by invitation,) as did Genl. Huntington, at the House of Mr. Brown, where I lodged, and who keeps a good Tavern. Drank Tea at the Mayor's (Mr. Sherman). Upon further enquiry I find that there has been abt. ———— yards of coarse Linnen manufactured at this place since it was established—and that a Glass work is on foot here for the manufacture of Bottles. At 7 o'clock in the evening many Officers of this State, belonging to the late Continental army, called to pay their respects to me. By some of them it was said that the people of this State could, with more ease pay an additional 100,000£. tax this year than what was laid last year.

Monday, 19th.

Left New-haven at 6 o'clock, and arrived at Wallingford (13 miles) by half after 8 o'clock, where we breakfasted, and took a walk through the Town. In coming to it we passed thro' East Haven about midway; after riding along the river of that name 6 miles, on which are extensive marshes now loaded with hay stacks—the ride is very pleasant, but the Road is sandy, which it continues to be within a mile of the Tavern (Carrington's, which is but an ordinary house,) at Wallingford. This and about five miles of the Road beyond—that is west of New-haven—is all the sand we have met with on the journey. These Sandy lands afford but ordinary Crops of Corn—nor have the Crops of this grain East of Stratford River appeared as heavy as on the West side of it. The Lands (Stone being less) are in part enclosed with Posts and Rails. At this place (Wallingford) we see the white Mulberry growing, raised from the seed, to feed the silkworm. We also saw samples of lustring (exceeding good) which had been manufactured from the Cocoon raised in this Town, and silk thread very fine. This, except the weaving, is the work of private families, without interference with other business, and is likely to turn out a beneficial amusement. In the Township of Mansfield they are further advanced in this business. Wallingford has a Church and two meeting houses in it, which stand upon high and pleasant grd. About 10 o'clock we left this place, and at the distance of 8 miles passed through Durham. At one we arrived at Middletown, on Connecticut River, being met two or three miles from it by the respectable Citizens of the place, and escorted in by them. While dinner was getting ready I took a walk round the Town, from the heights of which the prospect is beautiful. Belonging to this place, I was informed (by a Genl. Sage) that there were about 20 sea vessels, and to Weathersfield, higher up, 22—and to Hartford the like number—other places on the River have their proportion,—the whole amounting to about 10,000 Tons.

The Country hereabouts is beautiful and the Lands good. An average Crop of wheat from an acre of fallowed land is estimated at 15 bushels; sometimes they get as high as 25 and 30 bushs. to the acre from the best lands. Indian Corn from 20 to 40 bushls. pr. acre. Their exports are the same as from other places ; together with Potash. Having dined, we set out with the same Escort (who conducted us into town) about 3 o'clock for Hartford, and passing through a Parish of Middletown and Weathersfield, we arrived at Harfd. about sundown. At Weathersfield we were met by a party of the Hartford light horse, and a number of Gentlemen from the same place with Col⁰⋅ Wadsworth at their head, and escorted to Bull's Tavern, where we lodged.

TUESDAY, 20th.

After breakfast, accompanied by Col⁰⋅ Wadsworth, Mr. Ellsworth and Col⁰⋅ Jesse Root, I viewed the Woollen Manufactory at this place, which seems to be going on with spirit. Their Broadcloths are not of the first quality, as yet, but they are good ; as are their Coatings, Cassimeres, Serges and Everlastings ; of the first, that is, broad-cloth, I ordered a suit to be sent to me at New York—and of the latter a whole piece, to make breeches for my servants. All the parts of this business are performed at the Manufactory except the spinning—this is done by the Country people, who are paid by the cut.

Hartford is more compactly built than Middletown, and contains more souls ; the computed number of which amount to about dble. The number of Houses in Middletown are said to be 250 or 60—these reckoning eight persons to a house, would make two thousand at least. The depth of water which Vessels can bring to the last place, is about ten feet ; and is as much as there is over Saybrook bar. From Middletown to Hartford there is not more than 6 feet water. At Middletown there is one Episcopal and two Congregational Churches. In Hartford there is none of the first and 2 of the latter.

Dined and drank Tea at Col$^{o.}$ Wadsworth's, and about 7 o'clock received from, and answered the Address of, the Town of Hartford.

WEDNESDAY, 21st.

By promise I was to have Breakfasted at Mr. Ellsworth's at Windsor, on my way to Springfield, but the morning proving very wet, and the rain not ceasing till past 10 o'clock, I did not set out till half after that hour ; I called, however, on Mr. Ellsworth and stay'd there near an hour— reached Springfield by 4 o'clock, and while dinner was getting, examined the Continental Stores at this place, which I found in very good order at the buildings (on the hill above the Town) which belong to the United States.

The Barracks (also public property) are going fast to destruction, and in a little time will be no more, without re-
pairs. The Elaboratory, wch. seems to be a good building,
is in tolerable good repair, and the Powder Magazine, which
is of Brick, seems to be in excellent order, and the Powder
in it very dry. A Col⁰· Worthington, Col⁰· Williams, Ad-
jutant General of the State of Massachusetts, Gen. Shep-
herd, Mr. Lyman, and many other Gentlemen sat an hour
or two with me in the evening at Parson's Tavern, where I
lodged, and which is a good House. About 6 miles before
I came to Springfield, I left the State of Connecticut, and
entered that of Massachusetts. The Distance from Hartford to Springfield is 28 miles—both on Connecticut River.
At the latter the River is crossed in Scows set over with
Poles, and is about 80 rod wide. Between the two places
is a fall, and ten miles above Springfield is another fall, and
others above that again—notwithstanding which much use
is made of the navigation for transportation in flats of about
five tons burthen. Seven miles on this side Hartford is
Windsor, a tolerable pleasant but not a large village. Between Windsor and Suffield you pass through a level, barren and uncultivated plain for several miles. Suffield
stands high and pleasant—the Ld. good. From hence you
descend again into another plain, where the lands being
good are much better cultivated. The whole Road from
Hartford to Springfield is level and good, except being too
sandy in places—and the Fields enclosed with Posts and
Rails generally, there not being much stone. The Crops
of Corn, except on the Interval Lands on the River, are
more indifferent (tho' not bad) in the Eastern than we

found them in the Western part of the State of Connecticut.

There is a great equality in the People of this State. Few or no opulent men—and no poor—great similitude in their buildings—the general fashion of which is a Chimney (always of Stone or Brick) and door in the middle, with a stair case fronting the latter, running up by the side of the latter [former?]—two flush stories with a very good show of sash and glass windows—the size generally is from 30 to 50 feet in length, and from 20 to 30 in width, exclusive of a back shed, which seems to be added as the family encreases.

The farms, by the contiguity of the Houses, are small, not averaging more than 100 acres. These are worked chiefly by oxen, (which have no other feed than hay,) with a horse and sometimes two before them, both in Plow and Cart. In their light lands and in their sleighs they work Horses, but find them much more expensive than oxen. Springfield is on the East side of Connecticut River; before you come to which a large branch of it called Agawam is crossed by a Bridge. It stands under the Hill on the interval Land, and has only one Meeting house—28 miles frm. Hartfd.

THURSDAY, 22d.

Set out at 7 o'clock; and for the first 8 miles rid over an almost uninhabited Pine plain; much mixed with sand. Then a little before the road descends to Chicopee river it is hilly, rocky and steep, and continues so for several miles; the Country being Stony and Barren; with a mixture of Pine and Oak till we came to Palmer, at the House of one Scott, where we breakfasted; and where the land, though far from good, began to mend; to this is called 15 miles—among these Pines, are Ponds of fresh water.

From Palmer to Brookfield, to one Hitchcock's, is 15 miles; part of which is pretty good, and part (crossing the Hills) very bad; but when over, the ground begins to get tolerably good and the Country better cultivated, tho' the Crops of Corn do not look well and have been injured, it is said, by an early frost in September. A beautiful fresh water pond and large, is in the Plain of Brookland. [Brookfield?] The fashion of the Houses are more diversified than in Connecticut, though many are built in their style. The Inclosures have but indifferent fences; wood or stone according as the Country abounds with the latter—of which it is full after passing the pine levels. At Brookland [Brookfield] we fed the Horses and dispatched an Express which was sent to me by Govr. Hancock—giving notice of the measures he was about to pursue for my reception on the Road, and in Boston—with a request to lodge at his House.

Continued on to Spencer, 10 miles further, through pretty good roads, and lodged at the House of one Jenks, who keeps a pretty good Tavern.

Friday, 23d.

Commenced our course with the Sun, and passing through Leicester, met some Gentlemen of the Town of Worcester, on the line between it and the former to escort us. Arrived about 10 o'clock at the House of   where we breakfasted—distant from Spencer 12 miles. Here we were received by a handsome Company of Militia Artillery in Uniform, who saluted with 13 Guns on our Entry and departure. At this place also we met a Committee from the Town of Boston, and an Aid of Majr. Genl. Brooks, of the Middlesex Militia, who had proceeded to this place in order to make some arrangements of Military and other Parade on my way to, and in the Town of, Boston ; and to fix with me on the hours at which I should pass through Cambridge, and enter Boston. Finding this ceremony was not to be avoided, though I had made every effort to do it, I named the hour of ten to pass the Militia of the above County at Cambridge—and the hour of 12 for my entrance into Boston, desiring Major Hale, however, to inform Genl. Brooks'[4] that as I conceived there was an impropriety in my *reviewing* the Militia, or seeing them perform manœuvres, otherwise than as a private man, I could do no more than pass along the line ; which, if he thought proper, might be under arms to receive me at that time. These matters being settled, the Committee and the Aid (Col°· Hale) set forward on their return—and after breakfast I followed. The same Gentlemen who had escorted me into, conducting me out of Town. On the Line between Worcester and Middlesex I was met by a Troop of light Horse

---

[14] John Brooks was an active military officer in the Massachusetts line, during the whole war for independence. He was major-general of the militia of his county for many years; and when the war with England commenced in 1812, he was appointed adjutant-general of Massachusetts. He was elected Governor of that State in 1816, and was continued in office, by re-election, seven years.

belonging to the latter, who Escorted me to Marlborough, (16 miles) where we dined, and thence to Weston (14 more where we lodged.)   At Marlborough we met Mr. Jonathan Jackson, the Marshall of this State, who proposed to attend me whilst I remained in it.   A good part of the Road from Spencer to Worcester is Hilly, and except a little nearest the latter, very stoney.   From Worcester to Marlborough the road is uneven but not bad—and from Marlborh. to Weston it is leveller, with more sand.   Between Worcester and Marlborough the Town of Shrewsbury is passed— and between Marlborough and Weston you go through Sudbury.   The Country about Worcester and onwards towards Boston is better improved and the lands of better quality than we travelled through yesterday.   The Crops it is said have been good.   Indian Corn, Rye, Buckwheat and grass—with Beef, Cattle and Pork, are the produce of their Farms.

Saturday, 24th.

Dressed by Seven o'clock, and set out at eight—at ten we arrived in Cambridge, according to appointment; but most of the Militia having a distance to come, were not in line till after eleven; they made however an excellent appearance, with Genl. Brooks at their Head.   At this place the Lieut. Govr. Mr. Saml. Adams, with the Executive Council, met me and preceeded my entrance into town— which was in every degree flattering and honorable.   To pass over the Minutiæ of the arrangement for this purpose, it may suffice to say that at the entrance I was welcomed by the Selectmen in a body.   Then following the Lieut't.

Govr. and Council in the order we came from Cambridge, (preceeded by the Town Corps, very handsomely dressed,) we passed through the Citizens classed in their different professions, and under their own banners, till we came to the State House ; from which across the Street an Arch was thrown ; in the front of which was this Inscription— " To the Man who unites all hearts"—and on the other— " To Columbia's favorite Son"— and on one side thereof next the State House, in a pannel decorated with a trophy, composed of the Arms of the United States—of the Commonwealth of Massachusetts — and our French Allies, crowned with a wreath of Laurel, was this Inscription— " Boston relieved March 17th, 1776." This Arch was handsomely ornamented, and over the Center of it a Canopy was erected 20 feet high, with the American Eagle perched on the top. After passing through the Arch, and entering the State House at the S°· End and ascending to the upper floor and returning to a Balcony at the N°· End ; three cheers was given by a vast concourse of people who by this time had assembled at the Arch—then followed an ode composed in honor of the President ; and well sung by a band of select singers—after this three Cheers—followed by the different Professions and Mechanics in the order they were drawn up with their colours through a lane of the People, which had thronged abt. the Arch under which they passed. The Streets, the Doors, windows and tops of the Houses were crowded with well dressed Ladies and Gentlemen. The procession being over, I was conducted to my lodgings at a Widow Ingersoll's, (which is a very decent and good house) by the Lieut. Govr. and Council —

accompanied by the Vice-President, where they took leave
of me. Having engaged yesterday to take an informal
dinner with the Govr. to-day, but under a full persuasion
that he would have waited upon me so soon as I should
have arrived—I excused myself upon his not doing it, and
informing me thro' his Secretary that he was too much
indisposed to do it, being resolved to receive the visit.
Dined at my Lodgings, where the Vice-President favoured
me with his Company.

SUNDAY, 25th.

Attended Divine Service at the Episcopal Church, whereof Doctor Parker is the Incumbent, in the forenoon, and
the Congregational Church of Mr. Thatcher in the afternoon. Dined at my Lodgings with the Vice-President.
Mr. Bowdoin accompanied me to both Churches. Between
the two I received a visit from the Gov'r, who assured me
that indisposition alone prevented his doing it yesterday,
and that he was still indisposed; but as it had been suggested that he expected to *receive* the visit from the President, which he knew was improper, he was resolved at all
haz'ds to pay his Compliments to-day. The Lt. Gov'r and
two of the Council, to wit, Heath and Russell, were sent
here last night to express the Govr.'s concern that he had
not been in a condition to call upon me so soon as I came
to Town. I informed them in explicit terms that I should
not see the Gov'r unless it was at my own lodgings.[15]

---

[15] The conduct of Mr. Hancock on this occasion was severely cen-
sured, because it was generally believed that his sense of his own dignity as chief magistrate of Massachusetts, and not bodily illness, was

MONDAY, 26th.

The day being Rainy and Stormy, myself much disordered by a cold, and inflammation in the left eye,[16] I was prevented from visiting Lexington, (where the first blood in the dispute with G. Brit'n was drawn.) Rec'd the complim'ts of many visits to-day. Mr. Dalton and Genl. Cobb dined with me, and in the Evening drank Tea with Gov'r Hancock, and called upon Mr. Bowdoin on my return to my lodgings.

TUESDAY, 27th.

At 10 o'clock in the Morning received the visits of the

---

the cause of his omitting to call upon the President immediately after his arrival. The rebuke of official pride administered by Washington in his refusal to see Governor Hancock, except at the President's lodgings, appears to have decided the question of superior dignity in the mind of the Governor. For further illustration of this matter, see Governor Hancock's letters to Washington, dated respectively October 21st, and October 23d, 1789, in Sparks' *Correspondence of the Revolution*, Volume IV., pages 289–'90. In the first, he invited Washington to stay at his house, and said, "I could wish that the accommodations were better suited to a gentleman of your respectability;" and in the second, written after Washington had declined his invitation, Governor Hancock invited him to dine with him on Sunday, "*en famille*." He appears to have had his heart set on having the President call on him first.

[16] Sullivan, in his "Familiar Letters," says, that owing to some mismanagement in the reception ceremonials at Cambridge, Washington was detained a long time, and the weather being inclement, he took cold. For several days afterward a severe influenza prevailed at Boston, and its vicinity, and was called the *Washington Influenza*. It may not be inappropriate to mention that when, in 1843, President Tyler visited Boston, a similar influenza prevailed at New York, and throughout New England, which was called the *Tyler Grippe*.

Clergy of the Town. At 11 went to an Oratorio—and between that and 3 o'clock rec'd the Addresses of the Governor and Council—of the Town of Boston—of the President, &c. of Harvard College, and of the Cincinnati of the State; after wch. at 3 o'clock, I dined at a large and elegant Dinner at Fanuiel Hall, given by the Gov'r and Council, and spent the evening at my lodgings. When the Committee from the Town presented their Address it was accompanied with a request (in behalf, they said, of the Ladies,) that I would set to have my Picture taken for the Hall, that others might be copied from it for the use of their respective families. As all the next day was assigned to various purposes, and I was engaged to leave town on Thursday early, I informed them of the impracticability of my doing this, but that I would have it drawn when I returned to New York, if there was a good Painter there—or by Mr. Trumbull when he should arrive, and would send it to them.

WEDNESDAY, 28th.

Went, after an early breakfast, to visit the duck manufacture, which appeared to be carrying on with spirit, and is in a prosperous way. They have manufactured 32 pieces of Duck of 30 or 40 yds. each in a week; and expect in a short time to encrease it to   They have 28 looms at work, and 14 Girls spinning with Both hands, (the flax being fastened to their waste.) Children (girls) turn the wheels for them, and with this assistance each spinner can turn out 14 lbs. of Thread pr. day when they stick to it, but as they are pd. by the piece, or work they do, there is no other restraint upon them but to come at 8 o'clock in the morning, and return at 6 in the evening. They are the daughters of decayed families, and are girls of Character— none others are admitted. The number of hands now employed in the different parts of the work is   but the Managers expect to encrease them to   This is a work of public utility and private advantage. From hence I went to the Card Manufactory, where I was informed about 900 hands of one kind and for one purpose or another—all kinds of Cards are made ; and there are Machines for executing every part of the work in a new and expeditious man'r, especially in cutting and bending the teeth, wch. is done at one stroke. They have made 63.000 pr. of Cards in a year, and can undersell the Imported Cards—nay, Cards of this Manufactury have been smuggled into England.[17] At 11 o'clock I embarked on board the Barge of the Illustrious, Captn. Penthere Gion, and visited his Ship and the Superb, another 74 Gun Ship in the Harbour of Boston, about 4 miles below the Town. Going and coming I was saluted by the two frigates which lye near the wharves, and by the 74s after I had been on board of them ; as also by the 40 Gun Ship which lay in the same range with them. I was also saluted going and coming by the fort on Castle Isld.[18] After my return I dined in a large

---

[17] These were implements for carding wool by hand, and were used until several years after the close of the last war with Great Britain, when woollen manufactories became common in this country.

[18] This was called Fort Adams at that time. The island was ceded to the United States in 1799, when President Adams named the fortification *Fort Independence*. The present structure was erected during the years 1801, '02, '03.

company at Mr. Bowdoin's, and went to the Assembly in the evening, where (it is said) there were upwards of 100 Ladies. Their appearance was elegant, and many of them very handsome; the Room is small but neat, and well ornamented.

THURSDAY, 29th.

Left Boston about 8 o'clock. Passed over the Bridge at Charles-Town, and went to see that at Malden, but proceeded to the College at Cambridge, attended by the Vice-President, Mr. Bowdoin, and a great number of Gentlemen.

At this place I was shown by Mr. Willard, the President, the Philosophical aparatus, and amongst others Pope's Orary (a curious piece of Mechanism for shewing the revolutions of the Sun, Earth, and many other of the Planets), the library, (containing 13.000 volumes,) and a Museum. The Bridges of Charlestown and Malden are useful and noble—doing great credit to the enterprising spirit of the People of this State. From Boston, besides the number of citizens which accompanied me to Cambridge, and many of them from thence to Lynn—the Boston Corps of Horse escorted me to the line between Middlesex and Essex County, where a party of Horse, with Genl. Titcomb, met me, and conducted me through Marblehead (which is 4 miles out of the way, but I wanted to see it,) to Salem. The chief employment of the People of Marblehead (males) is fishing; about 110 vessels and 800 men and boys are engaged in this business. Their chief export is fish. About 5000 souls are said to be in this place, which has the appearance of antiquity; the Houses are old; the streets dirty; and the common people not very clean. Before we entered the Town we were met and attended by a Com'e, till we were handed over to the Select men, who conducted us, saluted by artillery, into the Town, to the House of a Mrs. Lee, where there was a cold collation prepared; after partaking of which we visited the Harbour, their fish brakes for curing fish, &c., and then proceeded (first receiving an Address from the Inhabitants) to Salem.

At the Bridge, 2 miles from this Town, we were also met by a Committee, who conducted us by a Brigade of the Militia and one or two handsome Corps in Uniform, through several of the Streets to the Town or Court House, where an Ode in honor of the President was sung—an Address presented to him amidst the acclamations of the People; after which he was conducted to his Lodgings. Rec'd the Compliments of many differt. classes of People, and in the evening, between 7 and 8 o'clock, went to an Assembly, where there was at least an hundred handsome and well dressed Ladies. Abt. nine I returned to my Lodgings.

The Road from Boston to this place is here and there Stoney, tho' level; it is very pleasant: from most parts you are in sight of the Sea. Meads, arable Land, and Rocky hills are much intermixed—the latter chiefly on the left. The Country seems to be in a manner entirely stripped of wood. The grazing is good — the Houses stand thick. After leaving Cambridge, at the distance of 4 miles, we passed through Mystick—then Malden—next Lynn, where it is said 175.000 pairs of shoes (women's, chiefly) have

been made in a year by abt. 400 workmen. This is only a
row of houses, and not very thick, on each side of the
Road. After passing Lynn you enter Marblehead, wch is
4 miles from Salem. This latter is a neat Town, and said
to contain 8 or 9000 Inhabitants. Its exports are chiefly
Fish, Lumber and Provisions. They have in the East In-
dia Trade at this time 13 Sail of Vessels.

Friday, 30th.

A little after 8 o'clock I set out for Newbury-Port; and
in less than 2 miles crossed the Bridge between Salem and
Beverly, which makes a handsome appearance, and is upon
the same plan of those over Charles and Mistick Rivers;
excepting that it has not foot ways as that of the former
has. The length of this bridge is 1530 feet, and was built
for about £4500, lawful money—a price inconceivably low
in my estimation, as there is 18 feet water in the deepest
parts of the River over which it is erected. This Bridge
is larger than that at Charlestown, but shorter by   feet
than the other over Mistick. All of them have draw
bridges, by which vessels pass. After passing Beverley, 2
miles, we come to the Cotton Manufactury, which seems to
be carrying on with spirit by the Mr. Cabbots (principally).
In this Manufactory they have the new Invented Carding
and Spinning Machines; one of the first supplies the work,
and four of the latter; one of which spins 84 threads at a
time by one person. The Cotton is prepared for these Machines by being first (lightly) drawn to a thrd, on the common wheel; there is also another machine for doubling and
twisting the threads for particular cloths; this also does

many at a time. For winding the Cotton from the Spin-
dles, and preparing it for the warp, there is a Reel which
expedites the work greatly. A number of Looms (15 or
16) were at work with spring shuttles, which do more than
d'ble work. In short, the whole seemed perfect, and the
Cotton stuffs w'ch they turn out, excellent of their kind;
warp and filling both are now of Cotton. From this place,
with escorts of Horse, I passed on to Ipswich, about 10
miles; at the entrance of which I was met and welcomed
by the Select men, and received by a Regm't of Militia.
At this place I was met by Mr. Dalton and some other
Gentlemen from Newbury-port; partook of a cold collation, and proceeded on to the last mentioned place, where
I was received with much respect and parade, about 4
o'clock. In the evening there were rockets and some other
fireworks—and every other demonstration to welcome me
to the Town. This place is pleasantly situated on Merrimack River, and appears to have carried on (here and
above) the shipbuilding business to a grt. extent. The
number of souls is estimated at 5000.

Saturday, 31st.

Left Newbury-port a little after 8 o'clock (first breakfasting with Mr. Dalton) and to avoid a wider ferry, more
inconvenient boats, and a piece of heavy sand, we crossed
the River at Salisbury, two miles above, and near that further about—and in three miles came to the line wch.
divides the State of Massachusetts from that of New Hampshire. Here I took leave of Mr. Dalton and many other
private Gentlemen who accompanied me; also of Gen'l

Titcomb, who had met me on the line between Middlesex and Essex Counties—Corps of light Horse, and many officers of Militia—and was rec'd by the President of the State of New Hampshire—the Vice-President; some of the Council—Messrs. Langdon and Wingate of the Senate—Col⁰· Parker, Marshall of the State, and many other respectable characters; besides several Troops of well cloathed Horse in handsome Uniforms, and many officers of the Militia also in handsome (white and red) uniforms of the Manufacture of the State. With this cavalcade, we proceeded, and arrived before 3 o'clock at Portsmouth where we were received with every token of respect and appearance of cordiallity, under a discharge of artillery. The streets, doors and windows were crowded here, as at all the other Places; and, alighting at the Town House, odes were sung and played in honor of the President. The same happened yesterday at my entrance into Newburyport—being stopped at my entrance to hear it. From the Town House I went to Colonel Brewster's Ta'n, the place provided for my residence; and asked the President, Vice-President, the two Senators, the Marshall, and Majr. Gilman to dine with me, which they did; after which I drank Tea at Mr. Langdon's.

NOVEMBER 1st.

Attended by the President of the State (Genl. Sullivan), Mr. Langdon, and the Marshall, I went in the forenoon to the Episcopal Church, under the incumbency of a Mr. Ogden; and in the afternoon to one of the Presbyterian or Congregational Churches, in which a Mr. Buckminster

Preached.[19] Dined at home with the Marshall, and spent the afternoon in my own room writing letters.

MONDAY, 2d.

Having made previous preparations for it, about 8 o'clock, attended by the President, Mr. Langdon, and some other Gentlemen, I went in a boat to view the harbour of Portsmouth; which is well secured against all winds; and from its narrow entrance from the Sea, and passage up to the Town, may be perfectly guarded against any approach by water. The anchorage is also good, and the shipping may lay close to the Docks, &c., when at the Town. In my way to the mouth of the Harbour, I stopped at a place called Kittery, in the Province of Maine, the river Piscataqua being the boundary between New Hampshire and it. From hence I went by the old Fort (formerly built while under the English government) on an Island which is at the entrance of the harbour, and where the Light House stands. As we passed this Fort we were saluted by 13 Guns. Having Lines, we proceeded to the Fishing banks a little without the Harbour, and fished for Cod; but it not being a proper time of tide, we only caught two, with w'ch, about 1 o'clock, we returned to Town. Dined at Mr. Langdon's, and drank Tea there, with a large circle of Ladies, and retired a little after seven o'clock. Before dinner I rec'd an address from the Town, presented by the Vice-President; and returned an answer in the Evening to

---

[19] The eminent Joseph Buckminster, D. D., the successor of **Dr.** Langdon.

one I had rec'd from Marblehead, and another from the
Presbyterian Clergy of the State of Massachusetts and New
Hampshire, delivered at Newbury Port; both of which I
had been unable to answer before.

TUESDAY, 3d.

Sat two hours in the forenoon for a Mr. . . . . .,[20] Painter,
of Boston, at the request of Mr. Breck, of that place; who
wrote Majr. Jackson that it was an earnest desire of many
of the Inhabitants of that Town that he might be indulged.
After this setting I called upon President Sullivan, and the
mother of Mr. Lear,[21] and having walked through most
parts of the Town, returned by 12 o'clock, when I was
visited by a Clergyman of the name of Haven, who presented me with an Ear and part of the stalk of the dyeing
Corn, and several small pieces of Cloth which had been
dyed with it, equal to any colours I had ever seen, of various colours. This Corn was blood red, and the rind of the
stalk deeply tinged of the same colour.

About 2 o'clock, I received an Address from the Executive of the State of New Hampshire, and in half an hour

---

[20] Gulligher. Doctor Jeremy Belknap, in his Diary, after mentioning that he, with other clergymen, called upon Washington, in Boston,
says—"N. B. While in the chapel, Gullager, the painter, stole a likeness of him from a pew behind the pulpit." He afterwards records—
"Gulliger followed General Washington to Portsmouth, where he sat
two and a half hours for him to take his portrait; which he did, and
obtained a very good likeness: after which he laid aside the sketch
which he took in the chapel; which, however, was not a bad one."
A fine engraving of Gulligher's portrait is published in "*Proceedings
of the Massachusetts Historical Society*," 1855–1858.

[21] Tobias Lear, the President's private Secretary.

after dined with them and a large company, at their assembly room, which is one of the best I have seen anywhere in the United States. At half after seven I went to the assembly, where there were about 75 well dressed, and many of them very handsome ladies—among whom (as was also the case at the Salem and Boston assemblies) were a greater proportion with much blacker hair than are usually seen in the Southern States. About nine, I returned to my quarters. Portsmouth, it is said, contains about 5,000 inhabitants. There are some good houses, (among which Col°. Langdon's may be esteemed the first,) but in general they are indifferent, and almost entirely of wood. On wondering at this, as the country is full of stone and good clay for bricks, I was told that on acct. of the fogs and damp, they deemed them wholesomer, and for that reason preferred wood buildings. Lumber, fish, and potash, with some provisions, compose the principal articles of export. Ship-building here and at Newburyport, has been carried on to a considerable extent. During and for some time after the war there was an entire stagnation to it; but it is beginning now to revive again. The number of ships belonging to the port are estimated at ——.

WEDNESDAY, 4th.

About half after seven I left Portsmouth, quietly, and without any attendance, having earnestly entreated that all parade and ceremony might be avoided on my return. Before ten I reached Exeter, 14 miles distance. This is considered as the second town in New Hampshire, and stands at the head of the tide-water of Piscataqua River;

46

DIARY OF WASHINGTON.

but ships of 3 or 400 tuns are built at it. Above (but in
the town) are considerable falls, which supply several grist
mills, 2 oyl mills, a slitting mill, and snuff mill. It is a
place of some consequence, but does not contain more than
1,000 inhabitants. A jealousy subsists between this town
(where the Legislature alternately sits,) and Portsmouth;
which, had I known it in time, would have made it necessary to have accepted an invitation to a public dinner, but
my arrangements having been otherwise made, I could not.
From hence, passing through Kingstown, (6 miles from
Exeter) I arrived at Haverhill about half-past two, and
stayed all night. Walked through the town, which stands
at the head of the tide of Merrimack River, and in a beautiful part of the country. The lands over which I travelled
to-day, are pretty much mixed in places with stone—and
the growth with pines—till I came near to Haverhill,
where they disappeared, and the land had a more fertile
appearance. The whole were pretty well cultivated, but
used (principally) for grass and Indian corn. In Haverhill
is a Duck manufactory, upon a small but ingenious scale,
under the conduct of Col°. . . . . . . At this manufactory
one small person turns a wheel which employs eight
spinners, each acting independently of each other, so as to
occasion no interruption to the rest if any one of them is
stopped—whereas at the Boston manufactory of this article,
each spinner has a small girl to turn the wheel. The looms
are also somewhat differently constructed from those of the
common kind, and upon an improved plan. The inhabit'ts
of this small village were well disposed to welcome me to
it by every demonstration which could evince their joy.

THURSDAY, 5th.

About sunrise I set out, crossing the Merrimack River at the town, over to the township of Bradford, and in nine miles came to Abbot's tavern, in Andover, where we breakfasted, and met with much attention from Mr. Phillips,[22] President of the Senate of Massachusetts, who accompanied us through Bellariki[23] to Lexington, where I dined, and viewed the spot on which the first blood was spilt in the dispute with Great Britain, on the 19th of April, 1775. Here I parted with Mr. Phillips, and proceeded on to Watertown, intending (as I was disappointed by the weather and bad roads from travelling through the Interior Country to Charlestown, on Connecticut River,) to take what is called the middle road from Boston. The country from Haverhill to Andover is good, and well cultivated. In and about the latter (which stands high) it is beautiful. A mile or two from it you descend into a pine level, pretty sandy, and mixed with swamps, through which you ride several miles, till you begin to ascend the heights on which the town of Bellarika stands, which is also pleasantly situated 10 miles from Andover. From hence to Lexington—eight miles—and thence to Watertown, eight more, the country is very pleasant, and the roads in general good. We lodged in this place at the house of a Widow Coolidge, near the Bridge, and a very indifferent one it is.

---

[22] Samuel Phillips, who was President of the Massachusetts Senate from 1786, until 1801, when he was chosen Lieutenant-Governor. He died in February, 1802.

[23] Billerica.

FRIDAY, 6th.

A little after seven o'clock, under great appearances of rain or snow, we left Watertown, and passing through Needham (five miles therefrom) breakfasted at Sherburn, which is 14 miles from the former. Then passing through Holliston, 5 miles, Milford 6 more, Menden 4 more, and Uxbridge 6 more, we lodged at one Taft's, 1 mile further; the whole distance of this day's travel being 36 miles. From Watertown, till you get near Needham, the road is very level—about Needham it is hilly—then level again, and the whole pleasant and well cultivated, till you pass Sherburne; between this and Holliston is some hilly and rocky ground, as there is in places onwards to Uxbridge; some of wch. are very bad. Upon the whole it may be called an indifferent road—diversified by good and bad land—cultivated and in woods—some high and barren, and others low, wet and piney. Grass and Indian Corn is the chief produce of the farms. Rye composes a part of the culture of them, but wheat is not grown on account of the blight. The roads in every part of this State are amazingly crooked, to suit the convenience of every man's fields; and the directions you receive from the people equally blind and ignorant; for instead of going to Watertown from Lexington, if we had proceeded to Waltham, we should in 13 miles have saved at least six; the distance from Lexington to Waltham being only 5 miles, and the road from Watertown to Sherburne going within less than two miles of the latter, (i. e. Waltham). The clouds of the morning vanished before the meridian sun, and the afternoon was bright and pleasant. The house in Uxbridge had a good external appearance, (for a tavern) but the owner of it being from home, and the wife sick, we could not gain admittance; which was the reason of my coming on to Taft's;[24] where, though the people were obliging, the entertainment was not very inviting.

SATURDAY, 7th.

Left Taft's before sunrise, and passing through Douglass wood, breakfasted at one Jacobs' in Thompson, 12 miles distant; not a good house. Bated the horses in Pomfret, at Col⁰· Grosvenor's, distant 11 miles from Jacobs', and lodged at Squire Perkins' in Ashford, (called 10 miles, but

---

[24] While President Washington was at Hartford, on his return, he wrote the following letter to Mr. Taft:

"HARTFORD, 8th November, 1789.

"SIR—Being informed that you have given my name to one of your sons, and called another after Mrs. Washington's family, and being moreover very much pleased with the modest and innocent looks of your two daughters, Patty and Polly, I do for these reasons send each of these girls a piece of chintz; and to Patty, who bears the name of Mrs. Washington, and who waited more upon us than Polly did, I send five guineas, with which she may buy herself any little ornaments she may want, or she may dispose of them in any other manner more agreeable to herself. As I do not give these things with a view to have it talked of, or even to its being known, the less there is said about the matter the better you will please me; but, that I may be sure the chintz and money have got safe to hand, let Patty, who I dare say is equal to it, write me a line informing me thereof, directed to 'The President of the United States at New York.' I wish you and your family well, and am your humble servant,

"GEO. WASHINGTON."

must be 12). The first stage, with a small exception, is intolerable bad road, and a poor and uncultivated country, covered chiefly with woods—the largest of which is called Douglass, at the foot of which, on the east side, is a large pond. Jacobs's is in the State of Connecticut, and here the lands are better, and more highly improved. From hence to Pomfret there is some woods and indifferent land, but in general it is tolerably good, and the farms look well. In and abt. Pomfret they are fine, and from thence to Ashford not bad; but very hilly, and much mixed with rock stone. Knowing that General Putnam lived in the Township of Pomfret, I had hopes of seeing him, and it was one of my inducements for coming this road; but on enquiry in the town I found that he lived 5 miles out of my road, and that without deranging my plan and delaying my journey, I could not do it.

SUNDAY, 8th.

It being contrary to law and disagreeable to the People of this State (Connecticut) to travel on the Sabbath day—and my horses, after passing through such intolerable roads, wanting rest, I stayed at Perkins' tavern (which, by the bye, is not a good one,) all day—and a meeting-house being within a few rods of the door, I attended morning and evening service, and heard very lame discourses from a Mr. Pond.[25]

---

[25] Reverend Enoch Pond, who died in 1807. On his tomb-stone are inscribed these words—" Generous in temper, correct in science, and liberal in sentiment, the gentleman, the scholar, and the Minister of the Sanctuary, appeared with advantage in Mr. Pond."

Monday, 9th.

Set out about 7 o'clock, and for the first 24 miles had hilly, rocky, and disagreeable roads ; the remaining 10 was level and good, but in places sandy. Arrived at Hartford a little before four. We passed through Mansfield, (which is a very hilly country, and the township in which they make the greatest qty. of silk of any in the State,) and breakfasted at one Brigham's, in Coventry. Stopped at Woodbridge's in Et. Hartford, where the level land is entered upon, and from whence, through East Hartford, the country is pleasant, and the land in places very good ; in others sandy and weak. I find by conversing with the farmers along this road, that a medium crop of wheat to the acre is about 15 bushels—of corn, 20—of oats, the same —and in their strong and fresh lands they get as much wheat as they can rye to the acre—but in warm or sandy land the latter yields most. They go more, however, upon grazing than either ; and consequently beef, butter and cheese, with pork, are the articles which they carry to market.

Tuesday, 10th.

Left Hartford about 7 o'clock, and took the middle road (instead of the one through Middletown, which I went).— Breakfasted at Worthington, in the township of Berlin, at the house of one Fuller. Bated at Smith's on the plains of Wallingford, 13 miles from Fuller's, which is the distance Fuller's is from Hartford—and got into New Haven which is 13 miles more, about half an hour before sun-down. At this place I met Mr. Gerry,[26] in the stage from New York, who gave me the first cert'n acct. of the health of Mrs. Washington.

WEDNESDAY, 11th.

Set out about sunrise, and took the upper road to Milford, it being shorter than the lower one through West Haven. Breakfasted at the former. Baited at Fairfield; and dined and lodged at a Maj. Marvin's, 9 miles further; which is not a good house, though the people of it were disposed to do all they could to accommodate me.

THURSDAY, 12th.

A little before sunrise we left Marvin's, and breakfasting at Stamford, 13 miles distant, reached the Widow Haviland's, 12 miles further; where, on acct. of some lame horses, we remained all night. The badness of these roads having been described as I went, I shall say nothing of them now.

FRIDAY, 13th.

Left Mrs. Haviland's as soon as we could see the road, and breakfasted at Hoyet's tavern, this side King's-bridge, and between two and three o'clock arrived at my house at New York, where I found Mrs. Washington and the rest of the family all well[27]—and it being Mrs. Washington's night

---

[26] Elbridge Gerry, one of the signers of the Declaration of Independence, and then a member of Congress from Massachusetts.

[27] It will be observed that in this tour, the President avoided Rhode Island, that State and North Carolina having, as yet, refused to ratify

to receive visits, a pretty large company of ladies and gentlemen were present.

SATURDAY, 14th.

At home all day—except taking a walk round the Battery in the afternoon.

At 4 o'clock received and answered an Address from the President and Corporation of Dartmouth College—and about noon sundry visits.

SUNDAY, 15th.

Went to St. Paul's Chapel in the forenoon—and after returning from thence was visited by Majr. Butler, Majr. Meredith and Mr. Smith, So. Car'a. Received an invitation to attend the Funeral of Mrs. Roosevelt, (the wife of a Senator of this State) but declined complying with it—first, because the propriety of accepting any invitation of this sort appeared very questionable—and secondly, (though to do it in this instance might not be improper,) because it might be difficult to discriminate in cases which might thereafter happen.[28]

---

the Federal Constitution, and were considered as essentially foreign states. On the day when the President returned to New York, the new convention of North Carolina voted to ratify the Federal Constitution; and Rhode Island was admitted into the Union on the 29th of May following.

[28] The etiquette of the President's household, and his intercourse with the public at large, were matters of much greater moment than they might, at first thought, appear. The precedents of monarchy might not be followed in a simple Republic, and yet a certain dignity was to be preserved. The arrangement of official ceremonials con-

MONDAY, 16th.

The Commissioners,[29] who had returned from the proposed treaty with the Creek Indians before me to this city, dined with me to-day, as did their Secretary, Col⁰· Franks, and young Mr. Lincoln, who accompanied them.

TUESDAY, 17th.

The visitors at the Levee to-day were numerous.

WEDNESDAY, 18th.

Took a walk in the forenoon, and called upon Mr. Jay on business, but he was not within. On my return, paid Mr. Vaughan, Senr. a visit, informal.

Sent a Commission as District Judge of So. Carolina, to the Hon'ble William Drayton, of that State.

THURSDAY, 19th.

The following company dined here to-day, viz:—Mrs. Adams, (lady to the Vice-President,) Col. Smith and lady, and Miss Smith, Mrs. Adams's niece—Gov'r Clinton and

---

nected with the President, appears to have been chiefly left to Colonel Humphreys, a former aid-de-camp of Washington, and very recently Secretary of Legation at Paris. The customs which were established during Washington's administration concerning the levees, the President not returning visits, et cetera, have ever since prevailed; and the Chief Magistrate of the Republic is never seen in the position of a private citizen.

[29] General Lincoln, Colonel Humphreys, and David Griffin, late President of Congress.

lady, and Miss Cornelia Clinton[30]—and Maj. Butler, his lady and two daughters.

FRIDAY, 20th.

The visitors of gent'n and ladies to Mrs. Washington this evening were numerous and respectable.

SATURDAY, 21st.

Received in the afternoon the Report from the Commissioners appointed to treat with the Southern Indians—gave it one reading—and shall bestow another and more attentive one on it.

SUNDAY, 22d.

Went to St. Paul's Chapel in the forenoon—heard a charity sermon for the benefit of the Orphan's School of this city.

Had a good deal of conversation in the evening with the above Commissioners on the more minute part of their transactions at the Treaty with the Creek Indians—and their opinion with respect to the real views of Mr. McGillivray,[31] the principles of whose conduct they think is self-interest, and a dependence for support on Spain. They think also, that having possessed himself of the outlines of

---

[30] Miss Clinton afterwards married the Minister of the French Republic to the United States, Edmund Charles Genet.

[31] Alexander McGillivray was then head chief of the Creek nation. He was the son of a Creek woman by a Scotchman, who was a wealthy Tory in Georgia during the Revolution. His property was confiscated, and his son took refuge among the Creeks, and by reason of his superior talents, became " the beloved man," or head chief of that nation.

the terms he could treat with the United States upon, he wished to postpone the Treaty to see if he could not obtain better from Spain. They think that, though he does not want abilities, he has credit to the full extent of them, and that he is but a short-sighted politician. He acknowledges, however, that an alliance between the Creek Nation and the United States is the most natural one, and what they ought to prefer, if to be obtained on equal terms. A *free* post in the latter seems to be a favourite object with him.

MONDAY, 23d.

Rid five or six miles between breakfast and dinner. Called upon Mr. Vanberckel[32] and Mrs. Adams.

TUESDAY, 24th.

A good deal of company at the Levee to-day. Went to the play in the evening[33]—sent tickets to the following ladies and gentlemen and invited them to seats in my box,

---

[32] Peter J. Van Berckel, of Rotterdam, was the resident diplomatic agent of the United Netherlands, near the government of the United States. He died at Newark, New Jersey, on the 17th of December, 1800, at the age of seventy-seven years.

[33] The theatre was in John-street, north side, not far from Broadway. It was a small, rickety affair, and capable of holding only about three hundred persons. A German, named Feyles, was the leader of the orchestra. He composed the *President's March* for this occasion, and that tune was played at the moment when Washington and his friends entered the theatre. It was afterwards slightly altered, and has been known as *Hail Columbia* ever since. It was doubtless on this occasion that Wignell performed the part of Darby, in the interlude of *Darby's Return*, a play written by William Dunlap. Darby, an Irish lad, recounts his adventures in the United States and elsewhere.

viz:—Mrs. Adams, (lady of the Vice-President,) Genl. Schuyler and lady, Mr. King and lady, Majr. Butler and lady, Col⁰· Hamilton and lady, Mrs. Green—all of whom accepted and came, except Mrs. Butler, who was indisposed.

WEDNESDAY, 25th.

Exercised on horseback between breakfast and dinner— in which, returning, I called upon Mr. Jay and Gen. Knox on business—and made informal visits to the Gov'r, Mr. Izard, Genl. Schuyler, and Mrs. Dalton. The following company dined with me, viz :

Doctr. Johnson and lady and daughter (Mrs. Neely), Mr.

When he told of what befell him in New York at the inauguration of the President, &c., "the interest expressed by the audience," says Dunlap, "in the looks and the changes of countenance of the great man [Washington] became intense. At the descriptive lines :

> "' A man who fought to free the land from woe,
> *Like me*, had left his farm, a soldiering to go,
> But having gain'd his point, he had, *like me*,
> Return'd, his own potato ground to see.
> But there he could not rest. With one accord,
> He is call'd to be a kind of—not a lord—
> I don't know what; he's not a *great man*, sure,
> For poor men love him just as he were poor,'

the President looked serious ; and when Kathleen asked,

> 'How look'd he, Darby ? Was he short or tall ?'

his countenance showed embarrassment, from the expectation of one of those eulogiums which he had been obliged to hear on many public occasions, and which must doubtless have been a severe trial to his feelings." The President was relieved by Darby's declaration that *he had not seen him.*

Izard and lady and son, Mr. Smith (So. Carolina) and lady, Mr. Kean and lady, and the Chief Justice, Mr. Jay.

After which I went with Mrs. Washington to the dancing assembly, at which I stayed until 10 o'clock.

THURSDAY, 26th.

Being the day appointed for a thanksgiving, I went to St. Paul's Chapel, though it was most inclement and stormy —but few people at Church.

FRIDAY, 27th.

Not many visitors this evening to Mrs. Washington.

SATURDAY, 28th.

Exercised on horseback.

SUNDAY, 29th.

Went to St. Paul's Chapel in the forenoon.

MONDAY, 30th.

Went to the Play in the evening, and presented tickets to the following persons, viz :—Doctr. Johnson and lady, Mr. Dalton and lady, the Chief Justice of the United States and lady, Secretary of War and lady, Baron de Steuben, and Mrs. Green.

TUESDAY, DECEMBER 1st.

A pretty full Levee to-day—among the visitors was the Vice-President and all the Senators in town. Exercised on horseback between 10 and 12.

Read the papers relative to our affairs with the Emperor of Morocco, and sent them to Mr. Jay to prepare answers to them.

WEDNESDAY, 2d.

Exercised in the post chaise with Mrs. Washington—visited on our return the Vice-President and family—afterwards walked to Mr. King's—neither he nor his lady were at home, or to be seen.

THURSDAY, 3d.

The following gentlemen and ladies dined here, viz :— Gen. Schuyler, his lady and daughter, (Mrs. Ranselaer) Mr. Dalton and his lady, the Secretary of the Treasury and his lady, Gen. Knox and lady, and Mrs. Greene, Baron de Steuben, Col. Osgood, (Post Master Gen'l) and the Treasurer, Majr. Meredith.

FRIDAY, 4th.

A great number of visiters (gentlemen and ladies) this evening to Mrs. Washington.

The Governor of New Jersey, and the Speaker of the House of Assembly of that State, presented an Address from the Legislature thereof, and received an answer to it, after which they dined with me.

SATURDAY, 5th.

Exercised on horseback between 10 and 12 o'clock.

The Vice-President and lady and two sons—Col. Smith and lady, and his sister, and Mrs. Adams's niece, dined here.

SUNDAY, 6th.

Went to St. Paul's Chapel in the forenoon.

MONDAY, 7th.

Walked round the Battery in the afternoon.

TUESDAY, 8th.

Finished my extracts from the Commissioners' Report of their proceedings at the Treaty with the Creek Indians— and from many other papers respecting Indian matters and the Western Territory. A full levee to-day.

WEDNESDAY, 9th.

Walked round the Battery.

THURSDAY, 10th.

Exercised on horseback between 10 and 12 o'clock.

The following company dined here to-day, viz: Mrs. King and Mr. and Mrs. Few, Mr. and Mrs. Harrison, Mr. and Mrs. Wolcott, Mr. Duer, his lady, and Miss Brown, Mr. Griffin and lady, and Lady Christiana and her daughter.

FRIDAY, 11th.

Being rainy and bad, no person except the Vice-President visited Mrs. Washington this evening.

SATURDAY, 12th.

Exercised in the coach with Mrs. Washington and the two children, (Master[34] and Miss Custis,) between breakfast and dinner—went the 14 miles round.

SUNDAY, 13th.

Went to St. Paul's Chapel in the forenoon.

MONDAY, 14th.

Walked round the Battery in the afternoon.

TUESDAY, 15th.

Exercised on horseback about 10 o'clock—called on the Secretary for the Department of War, and gave him the heads of many letters to be written to characters in the Western Country, relative chiefly to Indian Affairs.

Visitors to the levee to-day were not very numerous, though respectable.

WEDNESDAY, 16th.

Dined with Mrs. Washington and all the family, (except the two children) at Governor Clinton's—where also dined the Vice-President, his lady, Col⁰· and Mrs. Smith, the

---

[34] George Washington Parke Custis, who was for a long time the last surviving executor of the Will of Washington. He died at Arlington House, near Alexandria, Virginia, on the 10th of October, 1857, at the age of seventy-six years.

Mayor (Col⁰· Varick) and his lady, and old Mr. Van Berkel and his daughter.

Thursday, 17th.

The following company dined here, viz : The Chief Justice of the U. States and his lady; Mr. King, Col⁰· and Mrs. Lawrence, Mrs. Gerry, Mr. Egbert Benson, Bishop Provost, and Doct. Lynn and his lady.

Friday, 18th.

Read over and digested my thoughts upon the subject of a National Militia, from the plans of the militia of Europe, those of the Secretary at War, and the Baron de Steuben.

Saturday, 19th.

Committed the above thoughts to writing, in order to send them to the Secretary for the Department of War, to be worked into the form of a Bill, with which to furnish the Committee of Congress which had been appointed to draught one.

Sunday, 20th.

Went to St. Paul's Chapel in the forenoon.

Monday, 21st.

Framed the above thoughts on the subject of a National Militia into the form of a Letter, and sent it to the Secretary for the Department of War.

Sat from ten to one o'clock for a Mr. Savage,[35] to draw my Portrait for the University of Cambridge, in the State of Massachusetts, at the request of the President and Governors of the said University.

TUESDAY, 22d.

A pretty full and respectable Levee to-day—at which several members of Congress, newly arrived, attended.

WEDNESDAY, 23d.

Exercised in the Post-Chaise with Mrs. Washington to-day. Sent the dispatches which came to me from the Assembly of Virginia, and from the Representatives of several Counties therein, respecting the state of the frontiers and depredations of the Indians, to the Secretary for the Department of War, requesting his attendance to-morrow at 9 o'clock, that I might converse more fully with him on the subject of the communications.

THURSDAY, 24th.

The Secretary of War coming according to appointment, he was instructed, after conversing fully on the matter,

---

[35] Edward Savage was a native of New England. He had painted in Philadelphia before going to New York in 1789. He was an indifferent painter and engraver; and John Wesley Jarvis, who was his pupil, soon exceeded his master in skill. He had a kind of museum and picture gallery in Greenwich-street, New York, for a while. He published a print called *The Washington Family*, which has been reproduced in lithography, in our day. It was engraved by Edwin, a skilful engraver, assisted by Jarvis.

what answers to return to the Executive of Virginia, and to the Representatives of the frontier counties.

FRIDAY, 25th—*Christmas Day.*

Went to St. Paul's Chapel in the forenoon.

The visitors to Mrs. Washington this afternoon were not numerous, but respectable.

SATURDAY, 26th.

Exercised on horseback in the forenoon. Chief Justice Morris and the Mayor, (Col°· Varick) and their ladies, Judge Hobart, Col°· Cole, Majr. Gilman, Mrs. Brown, Secretary Otis, and Mr. Beekley, dined here.

SUNDAY, 27th.

At home—all day—weather being bad.

MONDAY, 28th.

Sat all the forenoon for Mr. Savage, who was taking my portrait.

TUESDAY, 29th.

Being very snowing, not a single person appeared at the Levee.

WEDNESDAY, 30th.

Exercised in a carriage.

THURSDAY, 31st.

Bad weather and close house.

The Vice-President and lady, Col.º Smith and lady, Chan'r Livingston, lady and sister, Baron Steuben, Messrs. White, Gerry, Partridge and Tucker, of the House of Representatives, dined here to-day.

JANUARY, 1790.

FRIDAY, 1st.

The Vice-President, the Governor, the Senators, Members of the House of Representatives in town, foreign public characters, and all the respectable citizens, came between the hours of 12 and 3 o'clock, to pay the compliments of the season to me—and in the afternoon a great number of gentlemen and ladies visited Mrs. Washington on the same occasion.

SATURDAY, 2d.

Exercised in the carriage with Mrs. Washington. Read the report of the Secretary of the Treasury respecting the state of his Department and proposed plans of finance.— Drank tea at the Chief Justice's of the U. States.

SUNDAY, 3d.

Went to St. Paul's Chapel.

MONDAY, 4th.

Informed the President of the Senate, and Speaker of the House of Representatives that I had some oral communications to make to Congress when each house had a quorum, and desired to be informed thereof—and of the time and place they would receive them.[36]

Walked round the Battery in the afternoon.

Received a report from the Secretary at War respecting the state of the frontiers and Indian affairs, with other matters which I ordered to be laid before Congress, as part of the papers which will be referred to in my speech to that body.

TUESDAY, 5th.

Several Members of Congress called in the forenoon to pay their respects on their arrival in town, but though a respectable Levee, at the usual hour, three o'clock, the visitors were not numerous.

WEDNESDAY, 6th.

Sat from half after 8 o'clock till 10 for the portrait painter, Mr. Savage, to finish the picture of me which he had begun for the University of Cambridge.

In the afternoon walked around the Battery.

Miss Anne Brown stayed here, on a visit to Mrs. Washington, to a family dinner.

THURSDAY, 7th.

About one o'clock rec'd a Committee from both Houses

---

[36] The second session of the first Congress commenced on the fourth day of January, 1790. Ten members only of the Senate having answered to their names, the Senate was adjourned for want of a quorum. A quorum of both houses appeared on the 6th.

of Congress,[37] informing me that each had made a house, and would be ready at any time I should appoint to receive the communications I had to make in the Senate Chamber. Named to-morrow, 11 o'clock, for this purpose.

The following gentlemen dined here, viz: Messrs. Langdon, Wingate, Strong and Few, of the Senate, the Speaker, Genl. Muhlenberg and Scott, of Pennsylvania, Judge Livermore and Foster, of New Hampshire, Aimes and Thatcher and Goodhue, of Massachusetts, Mr. Burke, of South Carolina, and Mr. Baldwin, of Georgia.

FRIDAY, 8th.

According to appointment, at 11 o'clock, I set out for the City Hall in my coach, preceded by Colonel Humphreys and Majr. Jackson in uniform, (on my two white horses) and followed by Messrs. Lear and Nelson, in my chariot, and Mr. Lewis, on horseback, following them. In their rear was the Chief Justice of the United States and Secretary of the Treasury and War Departments, in their respective carriages, and in the order they are named. At the outer door of the hall I was met by the door-keepers of the Senate and House, and conducted to the door of the Senate Chamber; and passing from thence to the Chair through the Senate on the right, and House of Representatives on the left, I took my seat. The gentlemen who attended me followed and took their stand behind the Senators; the whole rising as I entered. After being seated, at

---

[37] Messrs. Strong and Izard on the part of the Senate, and Messrs. Gilman, Ames, and Seney, in behalf of the House of Representatives.

which time the members of both Houses also sat, I rose, (as they also did) and made my speech; delivering one copy to the President of the Senate, and another to the Speaker of the House of Representatives—after which, and being a few moments seated, I retired, bowing on each side to the assembly (who stood) as I passed, and descending to the lower hall, attended as before, I returned with them to my house.

In the evening a *great* number of ladies, and many gentlemen visited Mrs. Washington.

On this occasion I was dressed in a suit of clothes made at the Woolen Manufactory at Hartford, as the buttons also were.

SATURDAY, 9th.

Exercised with Mrs. Washington and the children in the coach the 14 miles round.[38] In the afternoon walked round the Battery.

SUNDAY, 10th.

Went to St. Paul's Chapel in the forenoon—wrote private letters in the afternoon for the Southern mail.

MONDAY, 11th.

Sent my instructions to the Commissioners (appointed to negotiate a Treaty with the Creek Indians) with the report

---

[38] The route was by the old King's-Bridge road, which passed over Murray Hill, where Lexington Avenue now does, to McGowan's Pass at about One hundred and eighth street; then across on a line with the Harlem river to Bloomingdale, and so down on the westerly side of the island.

of their proceedings, to the Senate by the Secretary at War, previous to their being laid before them and the other house in their legislative capacities.

Also communicated to both Houses, transcripts of the adoption and ratification of the New Constitution by the State of North Carolina, with copies of the letter from His Excellency, Saml. Johnson, President of the Convention, enclosing the same. These were sent by my private Secretary, Mr. Lear.

TUESDAY, 12th.

Exercised on horseback between 10 and 12—ye riding bad. Previous to this, I sent written messages to both Houses of Congress, informing them that the Secretary at War would lay before them a full and complete statement of the business as it respected the negotiation with the Creek Indians—my instructions to, and the Commissioners' report of their proceedings with those people—the letters and other papers respecting depredations on the western frontiers of Virginia, and District of Kentucky. All of which was for their *full* information, but communicated in confidence, and under injunction that no copies be taken, or communications made of such parts as ought to be kept secret.

About two o'clock a Committee of the Senate waited on me with a copy of their address, in answer to my speech, and requesting to know at what time and place it should be presented. I named my own house, and Thursday next, at 11 o'clock, for the purpose.

Just before Levee hour, a Committee from the House of

Representatives called upon me to know when and where they should deliver their address. I named twelve o'clock on Thursday; but finding it was there wish that it should be presented at the Federal Hall, and offering to surrender the Representatives' Chamber for this purpose, by retiring into one of the Committee rooms, and there waiting until I was ready to receive it, I would consider on the place, and let them know my determination before the House should sit to-morrow.[36]

A respectable, though not a full Levee to-day.

WEDNESDAY, 13th.

After duly considering on the place for receiving the address of the House of Representatives, I concluded that it would be best to do it at my own house—first, because it seems most consistent with usage and custom—2d, because there is no third place in the Federal Hall (*prepared*) to which I could call them, and to go into either of the chambers appropriated to the Senate or Representatives, did not appear proper; and 3d, because I had appointed my own house for the Senate to deliver theirs in, and accordingly appointed my own house to receive it.

---

[39] As soon as the President and House of Representatives had retired, the Senate ordered the President's speech to be printed; also appointed a committee, consisting of Messrs. King, Izard, and Paterson, to report the draft of an answer to it. On the 9th, the House of Representatives took similar action, and appointed as its committee, Messrs. Smith, of South Carolina, Clymer, and Lawrence. Mr. King reported an address to the Senate on the 11th, which was accepted; and the following day similar action was had in the House.

THURSDAY, 14th.

At the hours appointed, the Senate and House of Representatives presented their respective addresses—the members of both coming in carriages, and the latter with the Mace preceding the Speaker. The address of the Senate was presented by the Vice-President—and that of the House by the Speaker thereof.

The following gentlemen dined here to-day, viz:

Messrs. Henry and Maclay, of the Senate—and Messrs. Wadsworth, Trumbull, Floyd, Boudinot, Wynkoop, Seney, Page, Lee, and Mathews, of the House of Representatives; and Mr. John Trumbull.

FRIDAY, 15th.

Snowing all day—but few ladies and gentlemen as visitors this evening to Mrs. Washington.

SATURDAY, 16th.

Exercised in the coach with Mrs. Washington and the two children, about 12 o'clock.

Sent the Report of the Post Master General relative to the necessary changes in that office to the Secretary of the Treasury, that it may be laid before Congress—or such parts thereof as may be necessary for their information.

SUNDAY, 17th.

At home all day—not well.

MONDAY, 18th.

Still indisposed with an aching tooth, and swelled and inflamed gum.

TUESDAY, 19th.

Not much company at the Levee to-day—but the visitors were respectable.

WEDNESDAY, 20th.

A Report from the Secretary at War, on the subject of a National Militia, altered agreeably to the ideas I had communicated to him, was presented to me, in order to be laid before Congress.

THURSDAY, 21st.

The above report was accordingly transmitted to both Houses of Congress by the Secretary at War, in a written message from me.

The following gentlemen dined here, viz:—Messrs. Elsworth, Paterson, Elmer, Bassett, and Hawkins, of the Senate—and Messrs. Sherman, Cadwalader, Clymer, Hartley, Heister, Smith, (Maryland) and Jackson, of the House of Representatives — and Major Meredith, Treasurer of the United States.

FRIDAY, 22d.

Exercised on horseback in the forenoon.

Called in my ride on the Baron de Polnitz, to see the operation of his (Winlaw's) threshing machine.[40] The

---

[40] The Baron de Poelnitz had a small farm in the vicinity of Murray Hill, where he tried experiments in agriculture. He wrote a pamphlet on the subject, and also suggested to Washington the propriety of es-

effect was, the heads of the wheat being seperated from the straw, as much of the first was run through the mill in 15 minutes as made half a bushel of clean wheat—allowing 8 working hours in the 24, this would yield 16 bushels pr. day. Two boys are sufficient to turn the wheel, feed the mill, and remove the threshed grain after it has passed through it. Two men were unable, by winnowing, to clean the wheat as it passed through the mill, but a common Dutch fan, with the usual attendance, would be *more* than sufficient to do it. The grain passes through without bruising and is well separated from the chaff. Women, or boys of 12 or 14 years of age, are fully adequate to the management of the mill or threshing machine. Upon the whole, it appears to be an easier, more expeditious, and much cleaner way of getting out grain than by the usual mode of threshing; and vastly to be preferred to treading, which is hurtful to horses, filthy to the wheat, and not more expeditious, considering the numbers that are employed in the process from the time the head is begun to be formed until the grain has passed finally through the fan.

Many and respectable visitors to Mrs. Washington this evening.

Saturday, 23d.

Went with Mrs. Washington in the forenoon to see the Paintings of Mr. Jno. Trumbull.

---

tablishing a farm under the patronage of the government. The Baron was the inventor of various agricultural machines. In a letter to him, written in December previous, Washington proposed to take some occasion "of seeing the manner in which the threshing machine operates." That occasion is here noted.

SUNDAY, 24th.

Went to St. Paul's Chapel in the forenoon.
Writing private letters in the afternoon.

MONDAY, 25th.

A Mr. Francis Bailey, introduced by Messrs. Scott and
Hartley, of Pennsylvania, and Mr. White, of Virginia, offered a paper, in the nature of a Petition, setting forth a
valuable discovery he had made of marginal figures for
notes, certificates, &c., which could not by the ingenuity
of man be counterfeited—requesting I would appoint some
person to hear and examine him on the subject; that if the
facts stated by him should appear well founded, he might
(being a printer, of Philadelphia) have the printing of all
that sort of the public business for which this discovery
should be found useful—and which he would do on as good
terms as any other printer, independent of the discovery
above mentioned, all the advantage he should expect from
which being to obtain a preference.

Read a letter from George Nicholas, Esq., of Kentucky,
to Mr. Madison, which he put into my hands for information of the sentiments of the people of that district.

The sentiments are

That in the late Convention held 2d Nov'r in that district, the most important characters of that party which
has always been in favor of a seperation, oppose the
agreeing to it at this time, upon a supposition that the
terms have been changed by Virginia, so as to make
them inadmissible in their present form. Their en-

emies say this cannot be their *true* reason: but be them what they may, the scale is turned against the seperation.

That he believes no late attempt has been made by either Spain or England to detach that district from the Union—but—

That Spain is playing a game which, if not counteracted, will depopulate that country, and carry most of the future emigrants to her territory. That they have established a new government, independent of New Orleans at the Natchez, and sent thither a man of character and abilities—who would not for *unimportant purposes* have accepted the appointment.

That this new Governor has put a stop to the reception of tobacco from the inhabitants of the United States— declaring that none shall be received into the King's stores, (where it used to be purchased and deposited,) except from Spanish subjects—and that these shall have ten dollars a hundred.

That other great advantages are held out to emigrants from the United States to settle in the Spanish Territory—such as a donation of lands, and a certain sum in money for each family.

That the consequences of restriction on one hand, and encouragements to settlers on the other, are obvious— the difference of religion and government are all that can make any man hesitate in his choice—and perfect liberty in both these the strongest assurances are given.

That the French inhabitants of that country, as well as future emigrants from the old States, will certainly go there.

That persevering steadily in this conduct will drain the Western settlements.

That these considerations ought to make the Federal Government take (he thinks) the most decided steps as to the right of navigating the Mississippi, and induce it to pay particular attention to the gaining the affections of the Western people.

That the steps hitherto taken with respect to them have had a contrary effect: no support having been given by the General Government, and the regulation of Indian Affairs having been placed in hands who were interested in a continuance of their depredations on the Kentucky district.

That if a trade is not established with them on such a footing as to supply their wants, that they will do this by plunder.

That the management of this business being in the hands of persons North-West of the Ohio, it is inculcated on the Indians of the same side of the river, that as the Kentuckians and they are separate people, and in seperate interests, they may war with the first, and not with them. That of this disposition and conduct there are sufficient proofs whenever it is found that the interests of the two sides clash.

That the Commissioners being always named from persons living on that (North-west) side of the river, and always holding the Treaties there, contributes greatly to establish in the Indian mind this opinion of their being a distinct people.

That the Kentucky district being 20 times as numerous as the inhabitants of the other side, ought to have as great a share in the management of Indian Affairs as the people on the other side have.

That he is well convinced the bulk of the people in that district are strongly attached to the Union, and that characters might be found there better qualified to manage the business than those in whose hands it is now placed.

That if it is not the desire of the New Government to lose *all* its friends in that quarter, a change must be made in this business. The Indians must be convinced that the Americans are all one people—that they shall never attack any part with impunity—and that in future there real wants will be supplied in time of peace. This is all they ask.

That they deny in positive terms what the officers on the north-west side of the river assert, viz:—that hostilities are always commenced by the people of the Kentucky district. Expeditions have and will be carried on across the river in revenge for depredations of the Indians, untill the Government takes up the matter effectually.

That Mr. Brown (to whom he has written) can inform in

what light they are considered by the officers on the other side of the river.

That the want of money, he knows, prevents the Government from doing many things which otherwise would be undertaken, but that need not stop the necessary steps—because, if sanctioned by it, they can raise any number of men and furnish any quantity of provisions that may be wanting, and will wait until their finances enable them to make satisfaction.

That he fears the Government have taken up an idea that that country can be defended by a few posts along the river—if so, it is a most erroneous one, for an army would scarcely supply the chain that would be necessary.

That the post at the mouth of Licking is considered by many in the district of Kentucky as a check upon the said district. To this he can only say, if they are treated as fellow-citizens, checks are unnecessary—but if it is intended to withhold from [them] all the benefits of good government, a little time will shew that, as heretofore, they have found the troops useless and faithless as friends, so in future they shall despise them as enemies.

That upon the whole, he shall close the subject with assurances that Government are deceived in the accounts they have had from that country—and that it is his opinion that the most serious consequences will follow

from its persisting in the measures which have been
pursued for some time past.[41]

TUESDAY, 26th.

Exercised on horseback in the forenoon.

The visitors at the Levee to-day were numerous and
respectable—among whom was the Vice-President and
the Speaker of the House of Representatives.

Read a letter handed to me by the Secretary of War,
from a Col. Daniel Smith, of Miro settlement, in the State
of North Carolina, in reply to one which was an answer to
a letter received from the said Smith respecting Indian affairs and state of the frontier of that part of the Union,
and giving (as he was required to do) an account of the
navigation of the river Tennessee and its waters—the communication between these and other waters—and the distances of places, as follow, viz :—

The distance between the settlements of white people
south of the French Broad River, (☞French Broad
is a branch of Holstein[42] River, on the south side,
which is a branch of the Tennessee,) and the Indians
at and in the vicinity of Chota, (a Cherokee Indian
town,) is about 12 miles.

---

[41] Kentucky was yet a district of Virginia. The people of the territory adopted a State Constitution in 1790, but the separation from
Virginia did not take place until 1792. Kentucky was admitted into
the Union on the first of June, that year.
[42] Holston.

He never passed down the Tennessee himself. That part of it on which Chota stands is a south fork of the Holstein—their junction is about 20 miles below Chota, from which the whole river is called ye Tennessee.

Boats of 7 or 8 tons burthen have frequently gone down the Holstein—and the water is sufficient for those of greater burden; but there is a place called the Suck, or boiling pot, where the river runs through the Cumberland Mountains, that is somewhat difficult, occasioned by the narrowness of the water and suddenness of the turn, that causes a rebound and kind of whirlpool; but many boats have passed it, and he has not heard of damage to any of them, nor has he been informed that there is any material difficulty in the navigation more than is common in rivers of that size, where there is no tide.

Between the Suck and the Muscle Shoals, he is sure there is not.

Supposes the distance by water from Chota to the last mentioned place, is between 3 and 400 miles; the width of the river is very unequal—generally about 500 yards, except at the Suck, where it is not half that width.

The nature of the river, for the most part, is to have a bluff on one side and low grounds on the other, (which is liable to be overflowed) alternately; the banks are woody, and the low grounds thick with cane.

The Cherokees may be classed into three divisions. The

valley settlements on the Tennessee above Chota, eastward of the Iron Mountain—those in the neighborhood
of Chota—and those in the neighborhood of Chicka-
mogga, (which is a creek running into the Tennessee,
on the south side, a few miles above Suck)—they have
detached villages besides—but the number of their
towns is unknown to him—nor can he say what number of souls they may consist of, but supposes of . . . .

Warriors, there may be about 2,000 or 2,500—and of
the three divisions, the Chickamoggas are perhaps
the most numerous.

Muscle Shoals have different accounts given of them by
people who have passed them—some say they are 30
miles, others not 15 in length—but all agree that the
river *there* is about 3 miles in width, very shallow, and
full of small islands occasioned by drift wood lodging
on the rocks, by which means mud and sand are
accumulated; the lowest shoal is accounted rather the
worst. It is not possible for a large boat to pass them
in ascending the river at any season, nor can they pass
down them but in time of a flood.

Occhappo Creek he had never heard of—nor has he understood there was any creek on the south side of the
river, near the Muscle Shoals, that was navigable, unless when the river was high. Seven or eight miles
below the Muscle Shoals, there was formerly a Cherokee village, at the mouth of Cold Water Creek, but
he never heard that it was navigable : 15 or 20 miles

below this again is Bear Creek, on which a small tribe of Delawares live.

From the mouth of Cold Water Creek, or Bear Creek, to the highest navigation of the Mobile, he has heard it accounted 60 miles, but cannot say that it is so; the head waters of the Mobile may be about half that distance from the Tennessee.

Miro is the name of the district on Cumberland that includes three counties. Nashville the name of the town where the Superior Court is held. From hence to the lower end of the Muscle Shoals is about 150 miles, nearly south.

Duck River, a north branch of the Tennessee, where the path which leads from Nashville to the Chickasaw Nation crosses it, is about 60 miles from the Cumberland settlement—about a south-west course. About 100 miles further on the same direction is the nearest Chickasaw towns—the mouth of Duck River by water, he supposes may be near 200 miles below the Muscle Shoals.

Cumberland Settlements are not very compact—they extend from the mouth of Red River, a north branch of Cumberland River, up to Bledsoe's Creek, being about 80 or 90 miles. The strength of the militia about 800—and increasing fast—thinks they may be now by the late emigrations 1,000.

From Nashville to Lexington is about 200 or 210 miles by land—and from Nashville to the Falls of Ohio is about 140 miles, by land.

From the mouth of the Tennessee up to the Muscle Shoals the navigation is good—equal to that of the Ohio below the Falls—the width of the river near half a mile, in places almost double—the distance about 400 miles.

Chickasaws have no towns on the Tennessee—the nighest they have to it is about 60 miles from, or a little below Bear Creek. Their principal towns he has understood are on the heads of a fork of the Mobile, and on the head of the Yazoos; the number of their warriors is about 800.

Choctaws lye farther to the southward than the Chickasaws, and are a numerous nation. They are in alliance with the Chickasaws, and he has heard their numbers estimated at 7 or 8,000—at least equal to those of the Creeks, though not so well armed.

McGillivray's communications with the Cherokees he conceives have a constant tendency to excite them to war against the frontiers of Georgia and North Carolina—or at least cautioning them to be on their guard against the white people, and infusing suspicions into the minds of them. The Creeks have wanted them to join in a war against the white people, but they have refused, and would be glad to see them humbled for the insolence with which they treat them.

It will be highly pleasing to his settlement—Miro—to hear that Congress will protect it.

WEDNESDAY, 27th.

Did business with the Secretaries of the Treasury and War. With the first respecting the appointment of Superintendents of the Light Houses, Buoys, &c., and for building one at Cape Henry. With the latter for nominating persons (named in a list submitted to me) for paying the military pensioners of the United States—and the policy and advantages (which might be derived from the measure) of bringing Mr. Alex'r McGillivray, Chief of the Creek Nation here, being submitted to me for consideration, I requested that a plan might be reported by which Government might not appear to be the agent in it, or suffer in its dignity if the attempt to get him here should not succeed.

THURSDAY, 28th.

Sent a letter (with an Act of the Legislature of the State of Rhode Island, for calling a Convention of that State, to decide on the Constitution of the Union,) from Governor Collins, to both Houses of Congress—to do which, was requested by the act, of the President.

The following gentlemen dined here, viz : the Vice-President, the Secretary of the Treasury—Messrs. Schuyler, Morris, Izard, Dalton and Butler, of the Senate; and Messrs. Smith, (South Carolina,) Stone, Schureman, Fitzsimmons, Sedgwick, Huger, and Madison, of the House of Representatives.

Friday, 29th.

Exercised on horseback this forenoon; during my ride, Mr. Johnston, one of the Senators from North Carolina, who had just arrived, came to pay his respects, as did Mr. Cushing, one of the Associate Judges—the latter came again about 3 o'clock, introduced by the Vice-President.

Received from the Governor of North Carolina, an Act of the Legislature of that State, authorizing the Senators thereof, or one of the Senators and two of the Representatives, to make (on certain conditions) a Deed of Session of their Western Territory, described within certain natural boundaries; and requesting that the same should be laid before the Congress of the United States.

Received also a letter from the Baron de Steuben, declarative of his distresses; occasioned by the non-payment or non-fulfilment of the contract which was made with him by the Congress under the former Confederation,[43] and requesting my official interference in his behalf. The delicacy of this case from the nature and long laboring of it, requires consideration.

The visitors to Mrs. Washington this evening were numerous and respectable.

---

[43] On the 13th of June, 1785, the Continental Congress resolved to pay Baron de Steuben the sum of $1,826, with the interest thereon. On the 27th of September following, a further sum of seven thousand dollars was voted to be paid to him. These sums were to be given in consideration of his services during the Revolution.

SATURDAY, 30th.

Exercised with Mrs. Washington and the children in the coach in the forenoon. Walked round the Battery in the afternoon.

SUNDAY, 31st.

Went to St. Paul's Chapel in the forenoon

Mr. Wilson, one of the Associate Judges of the Supreme Court, paid his respects to me after I returned from church.

Spent the afternoon in writing letters to Mount Vernon.

FEBRUARY, 1790.

MONDAY, 1st.

Agreed on Saturday last to take Mr. McCombs' house, lately occupied by the Minister of France, for one year from and after the first day of May next; and would go into it immediately, if Mr. Otto, the present possessor, could be accommodated; and this day sent my Secretary to examine the rooms to see how my furniture could be adapted to the respective apartments.

TUESDAY, 2d.

Exercised in the carriage with Mrs. Washington.

On my return found Mr. Blair, one of the Associate Judges, the Attorney-General of the United States, and Col. Bland here.

The Levee to-day was much crowded, and very respectable ; among other company, the District Judge and Attorney, with the Marshall and all the Grand Jurors of the Federal District Court, (and a respectable body they were) attended.

Sent (yesterday) the Deed of Session of the Western Lands, by the State of North Carolina, to the United States, to both Houses of Congress.

WEDNESDAY, 3d.

Visited the apartments in the house of Mr. McCombs— made a disposition of the rooms—fixed on some furniture of the Minister's[44] (which was to be sold, and was well adapted to particular public rooms)—and directed additional stables to be built.[45]

---

[44] One piece of furniture " fixed on" was a writing desk or secretary, and also an easy chair that was used with it. In his will Washington disposed of these as follows :

" To my companion in arms and old and intimate friend, Dr. Craik, I give my beaureau (or as cabinet-makers call it, tambour secretary) and the circular chair, an appendage of my study." These articles are now in the possession of the Rev. James Craik, of Louisville, Kentucky, a grandson of Dr. Craik. Drawings of them may be seen in Lossing's " Mount Vernon and its Associations," page 215.

[45] This was on Broadway, west side, a little below Trinity Church. It was subsequently occupied as an hotel, and was called *The Mansion House*. The residence previously occupied by the President was on Cherry-street, just out of Franklin Square. By the removal of some buildings at the junction of Pearl and Cherry streets, that house had a front on Franklin Square for many years. It was demolished in 1856.

THURSDAY, 4th.

Received from a Committee of both Houses of Congress, an Act entitled "An Act for giving effect to the several Acts therein mentioned, in respect to the State of North Carolina, and other purposes."

The following company dined here, viz : The Vice-President, the Chief Justice of the United States, Judges Cushing, Wilson, and Blair, of the Supreme Court, and Judge Duane, of the District Court; the Attorney-General of the United States (Randolph); the Marshall, Attorney, and Clerk of the District, viz : Smith, Harrison, and Troup ; Mr. Johnson and Mr. Hawkins, of the Senate, and the Secretaries of the Treasury and War Departments, to wit :— Hamilton and Knox.

FRIDAY, 5th.

Received from Doctr. Williamson, of North Carolina, a list of names whom he thought would be proper to fill the Revenue offices in that State. Submitted the same to the Senators of that State for their inspection and alteration.

SATURDAY, 6th.

Walked to my newly engaged lodgings to fix on a spot for a new stable which I was about to build. Agreed with . . . . . to erect one 30 feet square, 16 feet pitch, to contain 12 single stalls; a hay loft, racks, mangers, &c.; planked floor, and underpinned with stone, with windows between each stall, for £65.

The resignation of Mr. Harrison as an Associate Judge, making a nomination of some other character to supply his place necessary, I determined, after contemplating every character which presented itself to my view, to name Mr. Iredell, of North Carolina; because, in addition to the reputation he sustains for abilities, legal knowledge, and respectability of character, he is of a State of some importance in the Union—that has given *no* character to a federal office. In ascertaining the character of this gentleman, I had recourse to every means of information in my power, and found them all concurring in his favor.

SUNDAY, 7th.

Went to St. Paul's Chapel in the forenoon.

MONDAY, 8th.

Nominated officers for the Revenue department in North Carolina. Mr. Iredell as an Associate Judge; and *all those* who had been temporarily appointed during the recess of the Senate to fill resigned offices; likewise Major Samuel Shaw, as Consul for Canton, in China.

Sent the Bill which had been presented to me on Thursday last, back to the House of Representatives, with my approving signature.

TUESDAY, 9th.

A good deal of company at the Levee to-day.
Exercised on horseback in the forenoon.

WEDNESDAY, 10th.

Sat from 9 until 11 o'clock for Mr. Trumbull to draw my picture in his historical pieces.[46] Dispatched Commissions, and all the necessary Acts, to the Revenue officers in North Carolina.

THURSDAY, 11th.

Exercised on horseback in the forenoon.

The following gentlemen dined here, viz : Messrs. Leonard and Groal, of Massachusetts ; Huntington and Sturges, of Connecticut ; Silvester, of New York ; Sinnickson, of New Jersey ; Gale, of Maryland ; and Bland, Parker and Moore, of Virginia.

FRIDAY, 12th.

Sat from 9 o'clock until 11, for Mr. John Trumbull, for the purpose of drawing my picture.

A good deal of company (gentlemen and ladies) to visit Mrs. Washington this afternoon.

SATURDAY, 13th.

Walked in the forenoon to the house to which I am about to remove. Gave directions for the arrangement of the furniture, &c., and had some of it put up.

---

[46] These "historical pieces" were the battles of Trenton and Princeton. Mr. Trumbull had arrived from Paris in November, 1789, and proceeded to paint as many of the heads of the signers of the Declaration of Independence as were present in Congress, at the second session, which commenced in New York on the fourth of January, 1790. At the same time he painted the portrait of Washington on horseback, for his "historical pieces," above referred to.

SUNDAY, 14th.

At home all day—writing private letters to Virginia.

MONDAY, 15th.

Sat between 9 and 11, for Mr. John Trumbull.

Sent to both Houses of Congress a Letter from the President of New Hampshire, enclosing the adopted articles of amendments of the Constitution of the United States, proposed by the latter at its last session, to the States individually. Perused two letters to Col°· Hawkins, of the Senate, sent to me by the Secretary of War for my information. The one from a Lardin Clark, dated Nashville, Warren County, the 8th of Sept'r, 1789 ; the other from Brig'r Genl. Joseph Martin, dated Smith's River, Jan. 7, 1790. The first of these letters mentions that the loose and disorderly people that first settled the district in which he is, remove, as government (by means of the Superior Court) is extended amongst them, and supplied by persons of better character and morals. That the Spanish Governor of Louisiana is holding out every lure to invite the citizens of the United States to settle under that government. That a Doctor White, who has been some time at New Orleans, does not seem to like the government, and discourages our settlers from migrating to it till it can at least be seen what measures the government of the Union will take respecting the navigation of the Mississippi. That conventions which it had been proposed to hold in Kentucky, and other districts of the western country, for the purpose of addressing the old Congress on this subject, had been proposed for the same reason. That there was no appearance of giving up the Post of the Natchez to the United States, though it was within their territory; on the contrary, Roman Catholic Churches were built there, and provision made for newly arrived priests. That the Spanish Governor has said that it is not want of land that make them oppose our settlements, or which causes them to withhold the navigation of the Mississippi from us, but because they do not like our advancing in such numbers, and so fast upon them. In short, they act under the operation of fear and jealousy, though they will not acknowledge these to be the motives for their conduct. That it has been reported through the Western Settlements that Mr. Gardoqui had invited them to put themselves under the Spanish government, with assurances of peace and trade as consequences of it; and that Governor, by proclamation, had invited them to become inhabitants of Louisiana. That any person (he is informed) may take produce to New Orleans, paying 15 pr. ct. duty to the King. That the force (military) in the two Floridas consist of two regiments, of 600 men each; and he is told a third is ordered to be raised, to consist entirely of Spaniards by birth. That the district in which he is, populates fast and will soon make a State. And as the navigation of the Mississippi is essential to them, it must be obtained by treaty, or by force, or they must connect themselves with the Spaniards. That it is not supposed the two Floridas and Louisiana contain more than 20,000 souls. That the distance from Nashville to New Orleans by land (which he has traveled) is about 450 or 500 miles, and not a mountain and hardly a hill in the way. That this year he supposes they will make 300 hhds. of tobacco—for which $3\frac{1}{2}d.$ only is given, when the Spaniard gets 10 dollars pr. hd. wt.

The other letter from Gen. Martin encloses the report of a Committee of the Assembly of North Carolina, which had been appointed to examine into a correspondence between him and Mr. McGillivray, by which he stands acquitted of any intention to injure the United States, or any of them. Informs him that from tolerable good information, he has just heard that the Chickasaw Nation had made a stroke at the Chicamages Indians, and were driving all before them. That several women and children of the latter had run to the inhabitants of Little River for refuge. That he shall set out in a few days, and as soon as the particulars can be known will give information of them. Wishes to know whether Congress approves of this war or not. Thinks he can easily stop it, if it does not meet their approbation. But adds, their wars with one another may be the means of peace to our frontiers. Requests a hint on the subject by way of Richmond, directed to the care of the Post-master there.[47]

---

[47] This matter was in relation to Tennessee, which had belonged to North Carolina. It was erected into a Territory in 1790 (having been ceded to the United States, by North Carolina, in 1784), under the title of "Territory south of the river Ohio," as distinguished from the "North-western Territory." In 1789, the Legislature of North Carolina authorized its representatives in Congress to execute deeds of conveyance of Tennessee to the United States, which they did the following year. Tennessee was admitted into the Union in 1796.

TUESDAY, 16th.

Intended to have used exercise on horseback, but the weather prevented my doing it. Ride to my intended habitation, and gave some directions respecting the arrangement of the furniture.

The Levee to-day was thin.

Received some papers from the Secretary at War respecting a correspondence to be opened between Col. Hawkins, of the Senate, and Mr. McGillivray, of the Creek Nation, for the purpose of getting the latter, with some other chiefs of that nation to this place, as an expedient to avert a war with them. But, the commissioning a person to negotiate this business with McGillivray, without laying the matter before the Senate, and the expense of the business appearing to bring in question the *powers* of the President, I requested to see and converse with the Secretary of War, tomorrow, on this subject.

WEDNESDAY, 17th.

The Secretary attending ; and reference being had to the Act constituting the Department of War, and the Act appropriating 20,000 dollars for the expense of treating with the Southern Indians seeming to remove (at least in a degree) the above doubts, but not in an unequivocal manner, I desired him to take the opinion of the Chief Justice of the United States and that of the Secretary of the Treasury on these points, and let me know the result.

THURSDAY, 18th.

Sat for Mr. Trumbull from 9 o'clock till 10; after which exercised in the post-chaise with Mrs. Washington. On our return home called on Mrs. Adams, lady of the Vice-President.

The following company dined here to-day, viz :—Judge Cushing and his lady ; the Postmaster General and his lady, and Messrs. Boudinot, Griffin, Coles, Gerry, and White, and their ladies.

Sent a Message to the Senate with the copies of a letter from the Governor of Massachusetts, and a resolve of the Assembly of that State, respecting the disputed boundary between them and the British of Nova Scotia.

FRIDAY, 19th.

Exercised on horseback about 9 o'clock. Walked afterwards to my new house.

Received a Capt. Drew, Com'r of a British sloop of war, sent express to Sir John Temple, Consul-General of that nation in the United States.

The visitors this evening to Mrs. Washington were numerous and respectable.

SATURDAY, 20th.

Sat from 9 until 11, for Mr. Trumbull. Walked afterwards to my new house—then rode a few miles with Mrs. Washington and the children before dinner ; after which I again visited my new house in my coach (because it rained).

Sunday, 21st.

Went to St. Paul's Chapel in the forenoon—wrote letters respecting my domestic concerns afterwards.

Monday, 22d.

Set seriously about removing my furniture to my new house. Two of the gentlemen of the family had their beds taken there, and would sleep there to-night.

Tuesday, 23d.

Few or no visitors at the Levee to-day, from the idea of my being on the move. After dinner, Mrs. Washington, myself, and children removed, and lodged at our new habitation.

Wednesday, 24th.

Employed in arranging matters about the house and fixing matters.

Thursday, 25th.

Engaged as yesterday.

In the afternoon a Committee of Congress presented an Act for enumerating the inhabitants of the United States.

Friday, 26th.

A numerous company of gentlemen and ladies were here this afternoon.

Exercised on horseback this forenoon.

Saturday, 27th.

Sat for Mr. Trumbull this forenoon; after which exercised in the coach with Mrs. Washington and the children.

Sunday, 28th.

Went to St. Paul's Chapel in the forenoon. Wrote letters on private business afterwards.

MARCH, 1790.

Monday, 1st.

Exercised on horseback this forenoon, attended by Mr. John Trumbull, who wanted to see me mounted.

Informed the House of Representatives (where the Bill originated) that I had given my assent to the act for taking a Census of the People.

Also communicated to both Houses the application from the field officers of Harrison County, (made through the County Lieutenant, Col°· Duval,) for assistance, as they apprehend the season was near at hand when Indian depredations would be commenced. With these, some other papers respecting the Western Frontiers were sent.

Tuesday, 2d.

Much and respectable company was at the Levee to-day.

Caused a letter to be written to the Gov'r of St. Jago, respecting the imprisonment of a Capt. Hammond.

WEDNESDAY, 3d.

Exercised on horseback between 9 and 11 o'clock.

THURSDAY, 4th.

Sat from 9 until half after 10 o'clock for Mr. Trumbull.

The following gentlemen dined here to-day, viz :—the Vice-President, Messrs. Langdon, Wingate, Dalton, Strong, Ellsworth, Schuyler, King, Patterson, Morris, McClay, Bassett, Henry, Johnson, Hawkins, Izard, Butler, and Few, all of the Senate.

FRIDAY, 5th.

A very numerous company of ladies and gentlemen here this evening.

SATURDAY, 6th.

Exercised in the coach with Mrs. Washington and the children, and in the afternoon walked round the Battery.

Received a letter from the Governor of the western territory, dated at the Rapids of Ohio,[48] giving an account of the state of affairs in the western country.

SUNDAY, 7th.

At home all day—writing letters on private business.

MONDAY, 8th.

Sent to both Houses of Congress the Resolves of the Delaware State, to adopt and make part of the Constitu-

---

[48] Now Louisville, Kentucky.

tion of the United States, the amendments proposed by the General Government—except the first article of the said amendments, the consideration of which they postponed.

TUESDAY, 9th.

A good many gentlemen attended the Levee to-day—among whom were many members of Congress.

WEDNESDAY, 10th.

Exercised on horseback between 9 and 11 o'clock. On my return had a long conversation with Col⁰· Willet,[49] who was engaged to go as a private agent, but for public purposes, to Mr. McGillivray, principal chief of the Creek Nation. In this conversation he was impressed with the critical situation of our affairs with that nation—the importance of getting him and some other chiefs to this city—the arguments justifiable for him to use to effect this—with such lures as respected McGillivray personally, and might be held out to him. His (Col⁰· Willet's) going, was not to have the appearance of a governmental act—he, and the business he went upon, would be introduced to McGillivray by Col⁰· Hawkins, of the Senate, (from North Carolina,) who was a correspondent of M'Gillivray's—but he would be provided with a passport for him and other Indian Chiefs, if they inclined to make use of it; but not to part with it if they did not. The letter from Col Hawkins to

---

[49] Marinus Willet, one of the active "Liberty Boys," in New York, when the Revolution was kindling, and a meritorious officer during that war.

McGillivray was calculated to bring to his and the view of the Creek Nation the direful consequences of a rupture with the United States. The disposition of the general government to deal justly and honorably by them—and the means by which they, the Creeks, may avert the calamities of war, which must be brought on by the disorderly people of both nations, if a Treaty is not made and observed. His instructions relative to the principal points to be negotiated would be given to Col°· Willet, in writing, by the Secretary of War.

THURSDAY, 11th.

A letter from Arthur Campbell, Esqr., of Washington County, Virginia, to the Secretary at War, was put into my hands by the latter, containing the following information—the letter dated 6th Feb., '90 :

That half the Cherokee Nation would desire to remain neuter in case of a war between the United States and the Creek Indians, viz :—those in the neighborhood of Chota, and all those which are called the Middle Settlements. The towns on the Tennessee below Hiwassee, and those on the heads of the Caussa, would aid the Creeks.

That from the Long Island in Holstein to the Junction of French Broad, the navigation is equal to that of Monongahela between the mouth of Cheat and Pittsburgh—below it, it is exceeding good to where the river passes through Cumberland Mountain, a distance of about 150 miles by water. Here the river runs with great rapidity against a steep rock, which forms its bank and makes a short turn, and gives this place the name of the whirl; the river here being not more than the fourth of its common breadth —above and below it is very deep but not dangerous, with care.

That from this place the river runs with a gentle current southerly, near the foot of the Cumberland Mountain, on the west side for about 100 miles, (something east-wardly of this distance the mountain ends,) then it begins to turn northwardly 100 miles more to the upper end of the Muscle Shoals.

That these Muscle Shoals are gentle rapids for about 30 miles, and the difficulty lays in strangers missing the right channel—the river being 2 miles wide and full of small islands.

That the Creek landing on the Tennessee is about 80 miles below the whirl, from whence there is a good road to the Caussa, on the branches of which, and the Alabama river, (both waters of the Mobile) most of the upper Creeks live.

That below the Muscle Shoals a row-boat of any size may ascend the river with almost the same facility it passes downwards.

That from Nashville to the lower settlements on Hol-stein the new road is computed 180 miles. Miro is the name of the district.

That from Nashville to the Muscle Shoals is 70 miles,

That it is the upper Creeks *generally*, the Cherokees of the lower towns, to wit, Chickamaga, Nickajack and Crows Town, that give annoyance to the Southern settlements of Kentucky, the path through the wilderness, and the Holstein settlements.

That the Miro District (which contains all the Cumberland settlements,) can raise 800 good militia men— total number of inhabitants may be about 4,000, besides slaves.

That Washington District in North Carolina contains 4,000 militia, and Washington District in Virginia about 2,000 militia—the two latter mostly in Holstein Valley.

That Kentucky District has between 8 and 10,000 men.

That in his opinion a regiment of militia could be raised to go against the Southern Indians, to serve one company in six weeks after the officers should receive orders for the purpose, and that before the expiration of that time 560 regular troops could be enlisted to serve three years or better—call them rangers. The light infantry companies and troops of horse in the different western counties might be ordered into service agreeable to the existing laws of Virginia. Out of these a fine Ranging Regiment might be enlisted.

That the distances, as computed, from place to place, are as follow, viz:

From Lexington, in Kentucky,

 To Danville .... 30 miles.

  Green River .... 60 "

  Big Barren River .... 60 "

  Red River Station .... 40 "

  Nashville, on Cumb'd .... 25 "

  Muscle Shoals................ 70 "

           —— 285.

From Lexington to Crab Orchard........ 40 miles.

 To Cumberland Gap.............100 "

  The mouth of Hiwassee........ 70 "

  Big Shoemac Town (Cherokee).. 40 "

  Creek Towns................. 60 "

           —— 310.

From Nashville to Holstein—

 To Bledsoes Lick .... 30 miles.

  Big Salt Lick (Cumber'd) ...... 30 "

  Junction of the Holstein and Ten-

   nessee ....100 "

           —— 160.

From the mouth of Holstein, the direct way to the Creek Towns—

 To Hiwassee old Town (Cherokees). 40 miles.

  Big Shoemac................ 30 "

  Upper Creeks or Caussa Waters . 60 "

           —— 130.

The following gentlemen dined here to-day, viz :

Mr. Read, of the Senate, the Speaker, and following gentlemen of the House of Representatives, viz :—Messrs. Gilman, Goodhue, Aimes, Wadsworth, Trumbull, Benson,

Lawrence, Peter Muhlenberg, Wynkoop, Vining, Carroll, Contee, Madison, Page, and Sumpter—also Judge Bedford and Mr. John Trumbull.

FRIDAY the 12th.

Exercised in the Post chaise with Mrs. Washington from 10 o'clock till near 12.

Signed the Passport which was to be committed to Col°· Willet for Mr. McGillivray and other Chiefs of the Creek Nation of Indians, and other papers necessary for his setting out on this business.[50]

A Pretty numerous company of visiters this evening to Mrs. Washington's Levee.

SATURDAY, 13th.

Exercised about 11 o'clock with Mrs. Washington & the Children, in the coach.

SUNDAY, 14th.

Went to St. Paul's Chapel in the forenoon—wrote letters on private business afterwards.

---

[50] See Note, page 99. Also Diary, Wednesday, March 10th. Colonel Willet persuaded McGillivray to accompany him to New York. He was accompanied by twenty-eight principal chiefs and warriors of his nation, and was received with marked attention at Philadelphia and the seat of government. At the latter place the Tammany Society took a conspicuous part in the reception. McGillivray was chosen honorary member of the St. Andrew's Society of that city, his father being a Scotchman. A treaty was consummated during the visit, by which mutual concessions were made.

MONDAY, 15th.

Received an Address from the Roman Catholics of the United States, presented by Mr. Carroll of the Senate, Mr. Carroll & Mr. Fitzimmons of the House of Representatives and many others, Inhabitants of the City of New York.

Received a letter from the Executive of the State of Pensylvania, by the hands of a Mr. Ryerson, one of the Representatives of that State in Assembly, respecting the exposed state of the County of Washington—this letter I sent to the Secretary of War to be laid before Congress.

I also received from the Speaker of the Assembly of Pensylvania, an Act, adopting the amendments to the Constitution as proposed by Congress, except the first article thereof.[51]

And Mr. Few, Senator from the State of Georgia, presented me with the copy of an Address from that State requiring to knw. when it would be convenient for me to receive it in form. Finding it out of the usual style—State politics being blended therewith, I informed Mr. Few that

---

[51] Amendments to the Federal Constitution were proposed by the different States, but not one of them was of a vital character. Seventeen of the numerous amendments were finally agreed to by the House of Representatives, but these were reduced to twelve by the Senate. Two of them were important. A member pronounced the other ten "of no more value than a pinch of snuff, since they went to secure rights never in danger." In the course of two years these ten, only, received the sanction of the several States.

as soon as I could make it convenient to receive it He should have notice thereof.

Tuesday, 16th.

Exercised on horseback between 10 & 12 o'clock: previous to this, I was visited (having given permisn.) by a Mr. Warner Miflin, one of the People called Quakers; active in pursuit of the Measures laid before Congress for emancipating the Slaves :[52] after much general conversation, and an endeavor to remove the prejudices which he said had been entertained of the motives by which the attending deputation from their society were actuated, he used arguments to show the immorality—injustice—and impolicy of keeping these people in a state of Slavery; with declarations, however, that he did not wish for more than a gradual abolition, or to see any infraction of the Constitution to effect it. To these I replied, that as it was a matter which might come before me for official decision I was not inclined to express any sentimts. on the merits of the question before this should happen.

The day being bad, not may visiters attended the Levee. At it Mr. Smith of South Carolina, presented the copy of an Address from the Intendant and ——— of the City of

---

[52] In February, a petition from the yearly meetings of Quakers of Pennsylvania and Delaware, and seconded by another from New York, were presented in Congress, praying for the abolition of the slave trade. Another was presented the next day, from the Pennsylvania Anti-Slavery Society, signed by Dr. Franklin as president, on the same subject. These petitions, and proceedings thereon, produced much agitation in Congress and throughout the country, during the spring of 1790.

Charleston, and was told that I would receive it in form on Thursday at 11 o'clock.

WEDNESDAY, 17th.

Gave Mr. Few notice that I would receive the address of the Legislature of Georgia to morrow at half after ten o'clock.

Sent to both Houses of Congress the Ratification of the State of Pensylvania, of the amendments proposed by Congress to the Constitution of the Union.

THURSDAY, 18th.

At half past 10 I received the address of the Legislature of Georgia—presented by Mr. Few the Senator & the 3 Representatives of the State in Congress.

At 11 o'clock the address from the Intendant and Wardens of the City of Charleston was presented by Mr. Smith.

The following Gentlemen dined here—viz: Messrs. Livermore, Foster, Patridge, Thatcher, Sherman, Fitzimmons, Hartley, Seney, See, Burke, Tucker, Baldwin, Jackson & Mathews of the Representatives in Congress—and Mr. Otis Secretary of the Senate, and Mr. Beckley Clerk of the House of Representatives.

In the Evening (about 8 o'clk) I went with Mrs. Washington to the assembly where there were betwn. 60 & 70 Ladies & many Gentlemen.

FRIDAY, 19th.

Exercised on Horseback betwn. 9 and 11 o'clock.

Information being given by Mr. Van Berkel, that Mr. Cazenove[53] just arrived from Holland, and of a principal Mercantile House there had letters for me which he wished to deliver with his own hands and requested to know when he might be presented for that purpose. It was thought, before this should be done, it might be proper to know whether they were of a public nature, and whether he was acting in a public character. If so, then to let them come to me through the Secretary of State—if not, then for him to send them, that the purport might be known before he was introduced, which might be at the next Levee, when he might be received and treated agreeably to the consequence he might appear to derive from the testimonials of the letters.—It being conceived that etiquette of this sort is essential with all foreigners to give a respect to the Chief Magistrate, and the dignity of the Government, which would be lessened if every person who could procure a letter of introduction should be presented otherwise than at Levee hours in a formal manner.

SATURDAY, 20th.

Exercised in the Coach with Mrs. Washington and the Children.

---

[53] This gentleman was one of a company from Amsterdam, who purchased land in Central New York. The town of Cazenovia, in Madison county, founded in 1795, and the village of the same name incorporated in 1800, were named in honor of Mr. Cazenove.

SUNDAY, 21st.

Went to St. Pauls Chappel in the forenoon—wrote private letters in the afternoon.

Received Mr. Jefferson, Minister of State about one o'clock.[54]

MONDAY, 22d.

Sat for Mr. Trumbull for my Picture in his Historical pieces,—after which conversed for more than an hour with Mr. Jefferson on business relative to the duties of his office.

TUESDAY, 23d.

A full & very respectable Levee to day,—previous to which I had a conversation with the Secretary of State on the following points, viz—First with respect to our Captives in Algiers,[55] in which, after detailing their situation—the measures he had taken for their relief—and the train in

---

[54] Thomas Jefferson had been called to Washington's cabinet as Secretary of State, on his return from France, where he had resided as minister, for some time. After a tedious journey of a fortnight from Richmond, in Virginia, Mr. Jefferson reached New York on the 21st of March.

[55] At this time Algerine corsairs were committing great depredations upon commerce in the Mediterranean sea, and many seamen were made prisoners and sold as slaves. A treaty was finally made, by which tribute was to be paid to the Dey in consideration of his keeping his corsairs from molesting American commerce. In after years this degrading agreement was broken by the United States, and their commerce and seamen protected by cannon.

which the business was in by means of a Genl. ——— who is at the head of a religious society in France whose practice it is to sollicit aid for the relief of the unfortunate Christians in Captivity among the Barbarians, it was concluded betwn. us, that it had better remain in that train a while longer,—this person had been authorized to go as far as about £150 Sterlg. each, for the ransom of our Captives; but the Algerines demanding a much larger sum it was conceived that acceding to it might establish a precedent which would always operate and be very burthensome if yielded to; and become a much stronger inducement to captivate our People than they now have, as it is more for the sake of the Ransom than for the labour, that they make Slaves of the Prisoners. Mr. Short[56] was to be written to on this subject, and directed to make enquiry of this General ——— what his expectations of redemption are at present.

Second,—He is of opinion, that excepting the Court of France, there is no occasion to employ higher grades in the Diplomatic line than *Chargé des Affaires ;* and that these, by the respectibility of their appointments, had better be at the head of their grade, than Ministers Plenipotentiaries by low salaries at the foot of theirs. The reason of the distinction, in favor of a Minister Plenipo' at Versailles, is, that there are more Ambassadors at that Court than any other and therefore that we ought in some measure to

---

[56] Mr. Short, Secretary of Legation, was left by Mr. Jefferson in Paris, as virtual *Chargé d'Affaires* of the United States at the French Court. Washington afterwards appointed him to that office.

approximate our Representative—and besides, its being a Court with which we have much to do.

Third,—With respect to the appointment of Consuls he refers to a letter on the nature of this business—the places where necessary—and the characters best entitled to appointmts. which he had written on the subject, while in France, to the Secretary of Foreign affairs.

Fourth,—That it might be advisable to direct Mr. Charmichael[57] to Sound the Spanish Ministry with respect to the obstacles which had hitherto impeded a Commercial Treaty, to see if there was any disposition in them to relax in their Territorial claims & exclusive right to the Navigation of River Missisipi.

WEDNESDAY, 24th.

Prevented from Riding by the unfavourableness of the weather.

THURSDAY, 25th.

Went in the forenoon to the Consecration of Trinity Church, when a Pew was constructed, and set apart for the President of the United Sts.[53]

---

[57] Mr. Carmichael was the diplomatic agent for the United States, at the court of Madrid. He was specially charged with the negotiation of a treaty, that should secure to the citizens of the United States the free navigation of the Mississippi river, the lower portion then being under the control of the Spanish government. This was finally effected.

[58] The resolution to set apart a pew in Trinity Church, for the President of the United States, was adopted by the wardens and vestrymen on Monday, the 8th of February, 1790. The Right Rev'd Bishop

Received from the Senate their opinion and advice on the Papers which had been submitted to them respecting the Incroachments on the Eastern boundary of the United States, and the disputes consequent thereof.

And from a Comee. of Congress two Acts—one, for establishing the mode for uniformity in Naturalization of Foreigners—the other making appropriations for the support of Government for the year 1790. By this last was granted,

doll'rs	cents	
141.492	— 73	— for the Civil list.
155.537	— 72	— War Department.
96.979	— 72	— Invalid Pensions.
10.000	—	President for Contingent Services of Government.
147.169	— 54	—For demands enumerated by the Secrety. of ye Treasy. on wch. the light Ho. on Cape Henry is includd.
120	—	To Jehoiakim McToksin.
96	—	" James Mathers.
96	—	" Gifford Dally.
551.491	— 71.	Total amount.

Provoost was Rector, John Jay and James Duane were wardens. The vestrymen were Hon'ble William S. Johnson, Thomas Randall, Hubert Van Wagenen, John Lewis, Andrew Hammersley, John Jones, William Laight, James Farquhar, Charles Stanton, Robert C. Livingston, Mathew Clarkson, Nicholas Kortright, Alexander Aylesbury, George Dominick, Nicholas Carman, Moses Rogers, and Richard Harrison.

The following Company dined here to day—viz—The Chief Justice Jay & his Lady, Genl. Schuyler & his Lady, the Secretary of the Treasury and his Lady, the Secretary of War & his Lady & Mrs. Greene, the Secretary of State (Mr. Jefferson) Mr. Carroll & Mr. Henry of Senate, Judge Wilson, Messrs. Madison & Page of the Ho. of Representatives, and Col⁰· Smith Marshall of the District.

FRIDAY, 26th.

Had a further conversation with the Secretary of State on the subject of Foreign appointments, and on the Provision which was necessary for Congress to make for them— the result of which was that under all circumstances it might be best to have Ministers Plenipy. at the Courts of France and England (if any advances from the latter should be made) and Chargés des Affaires in Spain & Portugal—Whether it might be necessary to send a person in this character to Holland—one in the character of Resident—or simply a person well skilled in commercial matters among other characters being questionable, nothing finally was decided—but it was concluded that the Secretary's information to a Committee of Congress with whom he was to converse on the subject of the Provision to be made, that the salaries allowed to our Diplomatic characters was too low—that the Grades which wd. be fixed on, to transact our affairs abroad would be as low as they cd. be made without giving umbrage, that therefore, about 36.000 dollrs. might answer as a provision for the characters to the Courts before named—or that it might take forty-nine or 50.000 dollars if it should be found that the lesser grades will not answer.

The company this evening was thin, especially of Ladies.

SATURDAY, 27th.

Exercised in the coach with Mrs. Washington and the children.

SUNDAY, 28th.

Went to St. Paul's Chapel in the forenoon.

MONDAY, 29th.

Exercised on Horseback in the forenoon—and called at Col⁰· Walton White's.[59]

TUESDAY, 30th.

Exercised in the Post Chaise with Mrs. Washington.

The Company at the Levee to day was numerous & respectable.

WEDNESDAY, 31st.

Exercised on Horseback.

---

[59] Colonel Anthony Walton White, of New Jersey, one of the most distinguished of the cavalry officers in the Southern campaigns. Washington regarded Colonel White with peculiar friendship. On one occasion he presented him with a gold pen in a silver case. It is preserved as a precious relic by his grand-daughter, Mrs. Evans, who resides near New Brunswick, in New Jersey.

APRIL, 1790.

THURSDAY THE FIRST.

Received from a Comee. of both Houses of Congress—the following acts—viz :—" An Act to accept a cession of the " claims of the State of No. Carolina to a certain District of " Western Territory," and an " Act to prevent the exporta-" tion of Goods not duly inspected according to the Laws of " the several States."

Communicated to both Houses of Congress a letter from the Govr. of So. Carolina, enclosing the adoption of the amendments by that State agreeably to the recommendation of Congress.

The following Company dined here to day.—viz :—Governor Clinton, the Speaker of the Senate & House of Representatives of the State of New York, Judge Duane, Baron de Steuben and Mr. Arthur Lee. Mr. King of the Senate, and the following members of the House of Representatives—Mr. Leonard, Mr. Sedgwick, Mr. Grout, Mr. Van Rensalaer, Mr. Hathrop, Mr. Clymer, Mr. Heister, Mr. Stone, Mr. Williamson, Mr. Ash and Mr. Huger.

FRIDAY, 2d.

Deposited the above Acts in the Secretary of State's Office and informed the Houses of Congress thereof.

But a thin company this Evening, on acct. of the badness of the weather, & its being good friday.

SATURDAY, 3d.

Exercised in the Coach with Mrs. Washington and the Children.

Gave notice to the Senate House of Congress that I had given my assent to the act accepting the Cession of No. Carolina,[60] & to the other House that I had passed the Bill to prevent the exportation of Goods, not duly inspected according to the Laws of the several States, these being the Houses in wch. they respectively originated.

Received from the Governor of the State of New York three acts of its Legislature—one adopting the amendments (except the 2d.) proposed by Congress—another ceding the Light House, at the Hook, to the United States, and the third authorizing & commanding the Goalers throughout the State to receive & safe keep Prisoners committed under the Authority of the United States.

SUNDAY, 4th.

At home all day—unwell.

MONDAY, 5th.

Exercised with Mrs. Washington in the Post Chaise.

Sent duplicates of the Acts received (as above) from the

---

[60] North Carolina ceded to the United States the Territory now constituting the State of Tennessee, subject, however, to North-Carolina land-warrants already issued. In the act of cession was a restriction "that no regulation made or to be made by Congress shall tend to the emancipation of slaves."

Executive of New York to both Houses of Congress for their information; & deposited the originals in the Secretary of States Office.

Tuesday, 6th.

Sat for Mr. Savage, at the request of the Vice President, to have my Portrait drawn for him.[61]

The Company at the Levee to day was thin,—the day was bad.

Wednesday, 7th.

Exercised with Mrs. Washington in the Post-Chaise.

Thursday, 8th.

The following Company dined here—viz—of the House of Representatives—Mr. Gerry, Mr. Huntingdon, Mr. Cadwalader, Mr. Boudinot, Mr. Sinnichson, Mr. Scott, Mr. Gale, Mr. Parker, Mr. Moore, & Mr. Brown, of the Treasury Department, the Comptroller (Mr. Eveleigh,) the Auditor, (Mr. Walcot,) & the Register Mr. Nourse—and of the Commissioners of Accts. Genl. Irvine, and Mr. Kean—together with Mr. Gore, attorney for the District of Massachusetts.

Friday, 9th.

Exercised on Horseback in the forenoon.

Received the "Act for the encouragement of Arts from a Comee. of Congress.

---

[61] See Diary, Monday, 21st of December, 1789, and Note.

The company who visited Mrs. Washington this afternoon was very numerous both of Gentlemen & Ladies.

SATURDAY, 10th.

Exercised in the Coach with Mrs. Washington and the
Children—walked in the afternoon around the Battery and
through some of the principal Streets of the City.

In the afternoon the Secretary of State submitted for my
approbation Letters of credence for Mr. Short as Charge de
Affaires, at the Court of Versailles, & his own Letter to
Monsr. Montmorin, taking leave of that Court both directed to that Minister—also to Mr. Short on the subject of
our Prisoners at Algiers.—And at Night he submitted the
copy of a letter he had drafted to Mr. Carmichael, respecting the Governor of the Island of Juan Fernandez who had
been disgraced & recalled from his Government of that
Island for having permitted the ship Washington which
had suffered in a storm to put into that Port to repair the
damages she had sustained in it, & to recruit her wood
and water,—this ship belonged to Banel & Co. of Boston.

SUNDAY, 11th.

Went to Trinity Church in the forenoon—and several
private letters in the afternoon.

MONDAY, 12th.

Exercised on Horseback after which did business with
the Secretaries of the Treasury and War Departments.—

The latter was directed to authorize the Judge of the Western district Harry Innis to permit the County Lieutenants of that District to employ 4 scouts in each of the Frontier Counties for the purpose of discovering the movements of the Indians & giving the alarm in case they are about—the other Frontier Counties along the River Ohio East side above the Kentucky district was also authorized to keep out the same number of scouts.

The Secretary of State submitted the draught of a Report to me, which he was about to make to the House of Representatives in Congress consequent of a letter & other Papers which had been referred to him on the subject of coinage,—which report appeared to me to be sensible & proper.[62]

Tuesday, 13th.

Exercised on Horseback about 10 o'clock.

A good deal of Company at the Levee to day.

Received from the Joint Committee of Congress " An " Act furthr. to suspend pt. of an act to regulate the Col- " lectn. of the Duties imposed by Law on the Tonnage of " Ships &c. &c."

---

[62] Mr. Jefferson urged upon Congress the necessity of a national coinage, " to banish the discordant pounds, shillings, pence, and farthings of the different States, and to establish in their stead, the new denomination"—that is, the decimal currency, consisting of " a golden piece of the value of ten dollars, a dollar in silver, a tenth of a dollar in silver, and a hundredth of a dollar in copper." For full information on this subject, see " Statesman's Manual," vol. iv., edition of 1858, page 223.

WEDNESDAY, 14th.

Exercised in the Post Chaise with Mrs. Washington.

THURSDAY, 15th.

Returned the above Act (presented to me on Tuesday,) to the House of Representatives in Congress in which it originated with my approbation & signature.

The following Company dined here to day—viz—

The Vice President & Lady, the Chief Justice of the United States & Lady, Mr. Izard & Lady, Mr. Dalton & Lady, Bishop Provost & Lady, Judge Griffin & Lady Christina, Col⁰· Griffin & Lady, Col⁰· Smith & Lady, the Secretary of State, Mr. Langdon, Mr. King & Major Butler. Mrs. King was invited but was indisposed.

FRIDAY, 16th.

Had a long conference with the Secretary of State on the subject of Diplomatic appointments—& on the proper places & characters for Consuls or Vice Consuls.

After which I exercised on Horseback.

The Visiters of Gentlemen and Ladies to Mrs. Washington this evening were very numerous.

SATURDAY, 17th.

Exercised in the Coach with Mrs. Washington and the children.

SUNDAY, 18th.

At home all day—the weather being very stormy & bad, wrote private letters.

MONDAY, 19th.

Prevented from beginning my tour upon Long Island to day from the wet of yesterday and the unfavourableness of the morning.

Conversed with the Secretary at War on the formation of the Troops proposed, by the amendments in the Senate to be established.

TUESDAY, 20th.

About 8 o'clock (having previously sent over my Servants, Horses, and Carriage,) I crossed to Brooklyn and proceeded to Flat Bush—thence to Utrich[63]—thence to Gravesend—thence through ———— Jamaica where we lodged at a Tavern kept by one Warne—a pretty good and decent house,—at the house of a Mr. Barre, at Utrich, we dined,—the man was obliging but little else to recommend it.—He told me that their average Crop of Oats did not exceed 15 bushls. to the acre—but of Indian Corn they commonly made from 25 to 30 and often more bushels to the acre, but this was the effect of Dung from New York (about 10 cart load to the acre)—That of Wheat they sometimes got 30 bushels and often more of Rye.

The land after crossing the Hills between Brooklyn &

---

[63] New Utrecht, on the western end of Long Island.

flat Bush is perfectly level, and from the latter to Utrich, Gravesend and in short all that end of the Island is a rich black loam—afterwards, between ———— and the Jamaica Road, it is more sandy and appears to have less strength, but is still good & productive.—The grain in general had suffered but little by the openess, and Rains of the Winter and the grass (clover &c.) appeared to be coming on well, —the Inclosures are small, & under open Post & Rail fencing.—The timber is chiefly Hiccory & Oak, mixed here and there with locust & Sasafras trees,—and in places with a good deal of Cedar.—The Road until I came within a mile or two of the Jamaica Road, called the middle road kept within sight of the Sea, but the weather was so dull & at times Rainy that we lost much of the pleasures of the ride.

From Brooklyn to Flatbush is called 5 miles, thence to Utrich 6—to Gravesend 2—and from thence to Jamaica 14 —in all this day 27 miles.

Before I left New York this morning, I signed Commissions, appointing Mr. Carmichael Chargé des Affaires at the Court of Versailles,[64] & Mr. Short, Chargé des Affaires at the Court of Versailles which though not usually given to Diplomatic Characters of their Grades was yet made necessary in the opinion of the Secretary of State by an Act of Congress.

WEDNESDAY, 21st.

The morning being clear & pleasent we left Jamaica about eight o'clock, & pursued the Road to South Hemp-

---

64 This should read Madrid.

stead, passing along the South edge of the plain of that name—a plain said to be 14 miles in length by 3 or 4 in breadth withot. a Tree or a shrub growing on it except fruit trees (which do not thrive well) at the few settlemts. thereon.—The soil of this plain is said to be thin & cold, and of course not productive, even in Grass.—We baited in South Hempstead, (10 miles from Jamaica) at the House of one Simmonds, formerly a Tavern, now of private entertainment for money.—From thence turning off to the right, we fell into the South Rd. at the distance of about five miles where we came in view of the Sea & continued to be so the remaining part of the day's ride, and as near it as the road could run, for the small bays, marshes and guts, into which the tide flows at all times rendering it impassible from the hight of it by the Easterly winds.—We dined at one Ketchum's wch. had also been a public House, but now a private one—received pay for what it furnished—this House was about 14 miles from South Hempstead & a very neat and decent one.—After dinner we proceeded to a Squire Thompson's such a House as the last, that is, one that is not public but will receive pay for every thing it furnishes in the same manner as if it was.—

The Road in which I passed to day, and the Country here more mixed with sand than yesterday and the soil of inferior quality ;—yet with dung which all the Corn ground receives the land yields on an average 30 bushels to the acre often more.—Of wheat they do not grow much on acct. of the Fly but the crops of Rye are good.

Thursday, 22d.

About 8 o'clock we left Mr. Thompson's—halted awhile
at one Greens distant 11 miles and dined Harts Tavern
in Brookhaven township, five miles farther. To this place
we travelled on what is called the South road described
yesterday, but the country through which it passed grew
more and more sandy and barren as we travelled Eastward,
so as to become exceedingly poor indeed, but a few miles
further Eastward the lands took a different complexion we
were informed.—From Hart's we struck across the Island
for the No. side passing the East end of the Brushey Plains
—and Koram[65] 8 miles—thence to Setakit[66] 7 miles more to
the House of a Capt. Roe, which is tolerably dect. with
obliging people in it.

The first five miles of the Road is too poor to admit Inhabitants or cultivation being a low scrubby Oak, not more
than 2 feet high intermixed with small and ill thriven Pines.
—Within two miles of Koram there are farms, but the land
is of an indifferent quality much mixed with sand.—
Koram contains but few houses—from thence to Setaket
the soil improves, especially as you approach the Sound;
but it is far from being of the first quality—still a good
deal mixed with Sand.—The road across from the So. to the
No. side is level, except a small part So. of Koram, but the
hills there are trifling.

---

[65] Corum, near the centre of the town of Brookhaven.

[66] Setauket, one of the oldest settlements in Brookhaven.

Friday, 23d.

About 8 o'clock we left Roe's, and baited the Horses at Smiths Town at a Widow Blidenberg's a decent House 10 miles from Setalkat—thence 15 miles to Huntington where we dined—and afterwards proceeded seven miles to Oyster-Bay, to the House of a Mr. Young (private and very neat and decent) where we lodged.—The house we dined at in Huntingdon was kept by a Widow Platt, and was tolerably good.—The whole of this days ride was over uneven ground and none of it of the first quality but intermixed in places with pebble stone.—After passing Smiths-town & for near five miles it was a mere bed of white Sand, unable to produce trees 25 feet high; but a change for the better took place between that & Huntington, which is a sml. village at the head of the Harbour of that name and continued to improve to Oyster-bay about which the Sands are good—and in the Necks between these bays are said to be fine. It is here the Lloyds own a large & valuable tract or Neck of Land from whom the British whilst they possessed New York drew large supplies of wood[67]—and where, at present, it is said large flocks of Sheep are kept.

Saturday, 24th.

Left Mr. Young's before 6 o'clock and passing Musqueto Cove,[68] breakfasted at a Mr. Underdunck's at the head of a

---

[67] Lloyd's Neck was a great rendezvous for Tories during a part of the Revolution.

[68] Now Glen Cove.

little bay;[69] where we were kindly received and well entertained.—This Gentleman works a Grist & two Paper Mills, the last of which he seems to carry on with spirit, and to profit[70]—distc. from Oyster-bay 12 miles.—From hence to Flushing where we dined is 12 more—& from thence to Brooklyne through Newton (the way we travelled and which is a mile further than to pass through Jamaica) is 18 miles more. The land I passed over to day is generally very good, but leveller and better as we approached New York —the soil in places is intermixed with pebble, and towards the West end with other kind of stone, which they apply to the purposes of fencing which is not to be seen on the South side of the Island, nor towards the Eastern parts of it.—From Flushing to New Town 8 miles & thence to Brooklyn, the Road is very fine, and the Country in a higher state of cultivation & vegetation of Grass & grain forwarded than any place also, I had seen, occaisioned in a great degree by the Manure drawn from the City of New York,—before sundown we had crossed the Ferry and was at home.

Observations.

This Island (as far as I went) from West to East seems to be equally divided between flat, and Hilly land, the for-

---

[69] Henry Onderdonk's, upon the shore of the present Hempstead Harbor, at the village of Roslyn.

[70] This was the first paper-mill erected in the province, and was established by Andrew Onderdonk at about the middle of the last century. There is a tradition in the family that, on this occasion, Washington made a sheet of paper (it then being made by hand) and that it was preserved for a great many years.

mer on the South next the Seaboard, & the latter on the No. next the Sound.—The highland they say is best and most productive, but the other is the pleasantest to work, except in wet seasons when from the levelness of them they are sometimes, (but not frequently having a considerable portion of Sand) incommoded by heavy & continual rains.— From a comparative view of their crops they may be averaged as follows.—Indian Corn 25 bushels—Wheat 15— Rye 12—Oats 15 bushels to the acre.—According to their accts. from Lands highly manured they sometimes get 50 of the first, 25 of the 2d & 3d, and more of the latter.

Their general mode of Cropping is,—first Indian Corn upon a lay, manured in the hill, half a shovel full in each hole—(some scatter the dung over the field equally)—2d. Oats & Flax—3d. Wheat with what manure they can spare from the Indian Corn land—with the Wheat, or on it, towards close of the Snows, they sow Clover from 4 to 6 lb; & a quart of Timothy Seed.—This lays from 3 to 6 years according as the grass remains, or as the condition of the ground is, for so soon as they find it beginning to bind, they plow.—Their first plowing (with the Patent, tho' they call it the Dutch plow) is well executed at the depth of about 3 or at most 4 Inches—the cut being 9 or 10 Inches & the sod neatly & very evenly turned.—With Oxen they plough mostly. They do no more than turn the ground in this manner for Indian Corn before it is planted; making the holes in which it is placed with hoes the rows being marked off by a stick — two or three workings afterwards with the Harrows or Plough is all the cultivation it receives *gener-*

ally.—Their fences, where there is no Stone, are very indifferent; frequently of plashed trees of *any* & *every* kind which have grown by chance; but it exhibits an evidence that very good fences may be made in this manner either of white Oak or Dogwood which from this mode of treatment grows thickest, and most stubborn.—This however, would be no defence against Hogs.

SUNDAY, 25th.

Went to Trinity Church, and wrote letters home after dinner.

MONDAY, 26th.

Did business with the Secretaries of State, Treasury, and War,—& appointed a quarter before three to-morrow to receive from the Senators of the State of Virgna. an address from the Legislature thereof.

TUESDAY, 27th.

Had some conversation with Mr. Madison on the propriety of consulting the Senate on the places to which it would be necessary to send persons in the Diplomatic line, and Consuls; and with respect to the grade of the first—His opinion coincides with Mr. Jay's and Mr. Jefferson's—to wit—that they have no Constitutional right to interfere with either, & that it might be impolitic to draw it into a precedent, their powers extending no farther than to an approbation or disapprobation of the person nominated by the President, all the rest being Executive and vested in the President by the Constitution.

At the time appointed, Messrs. Lee & Walker (the Senators from Virginia) attended, & presented the Address as mentioned yesterday & received an answer to it.

A good deal of respectable company was at the Levee to day.

WEDNESDAY, 28th.

Fixed with the Secretary of State on places & characters for the Consulate—but as some of the latter were unknown to us both he was directed to make enquiry respecting them.

Sent the nominations of the officers in the Customs of North Carolina, and one in the place of Mr. Jacob Wray of Hampton in Virginia—who has requested to resign his appointment to the Senate for their advice & consent thereon.

, Received from the Secretary for the Department of War a report respecting the Sale of certain Lands by the State of Georgia;[71] and the consequent disputes in which the United States may be involved with the Chicasaws & Choctaw Nations ; part, if not the whole of whose Countries, are included within the limits of the said Sale. This report refers to the Act, of the Legislature of Georgia, by

---

[71] The first legislature of Georgia which convened under the Federal Constitution, undertook to sell out to private companies, the pre-emption right to large tracts of land westward of the Chattahoochee river. They sold five million of acres to the "South Carolina Yazoo Company," for the sum of $66,964, seven million of acres to the "Virginia Yazoo Company," for $93,742, and three and a half million of acres to the "Tennessee Yazoo Company," for $46,875. These transactions gave rise to much trouble afterwards.

which this Sale is authorized—and to the opinion of the Attorney General respecting the Constitutionality of the Proceeding—Submitting at the same time certain opinions for the consideration of the Presidt.

THURSDAY, 29th.

Received from the Joint Committee of Congress two Acts for my approbation & Signature—viz :—

One for "Regulating the Military Establisment of the United States," and the other, "An Act for the Punishment of certain crimes against the United States."

Fixed with the Secretary of State on the present which (according to the custom of other Nations) should be made to Diplomatic characters when they return from that employment in this Country—and this was a gold Medal, suspended to a gold Chain—in ordinary to be of the value of about 120 or 130 Guineas—Upon enquiry into the practice of other Countries, it was found, that France generally gave a gold Snuff-box set with diamonds; & of differt. costs ; to the amount, *generally*, to a Minister Plenipotentiary of 500 Louisdores—That England usually gave to the same grade 300 guineas in *Specie*—and Holld. a Medal & Chain of the value of in common, 150 or 180 guineas the value of which to be encreased by an additional weight in the chain when they wished to mark a distinguished character.—The Reason why a Medal & Chain was fixed upon for the American present, is, that the die being once made the Medals could at any time be struck at very little cost & the chain made by our artizans, which (while the first should be retained as a memento) might be converted into Cash.

The following Gentlemen dined here — viz — of the Senate, Messrs. Strong, Doctr. Johnston, Mr. Patterson, Mr. Morris, Mr. Carroll, Mr. Lee, Mr. Walker, Govr. Johnston, & Mr. Gunn—and of the House of Representatives, Mr. Sturges, Mr. Benson, Mr. Floyd, Mr. Scureman, Mr. Vining, Mr. Smith Maryland, Mr. Bland, and Mr. Sumpter.

FRIDAY, 30th.

Conversed with the Secretary of the Treasury, on the Report of the Secretary at War's propositions respecting the Conduct of the State of Georgia in selling to certain companies, large tracts of their Western territory & a proclamation which he conceived expedient to issue in consequence of it.—But as he had doubts of the clearness of the ground on which it was proposed to build this proclamation and do the other acts which were also submitted in the report—I placed it in the hands of the Secretary of State to consider & give me his opinion thereon.

Returnd. the Bills which had been presented to me by the joint committee of Congress on Thursday to the Houses in which they originated with my signature, though I did not conceive that the Military establishment of the one was adequate to the exigencies of the Government, & the protection it was intended to afford.

The Visitors to Mrs. Washington this evening were not numerous.

M A Y   1st.

Exercised in the Coach with Mrs. Washington & the children in the forenoon—& on foot in the afternoon.

Mr. Alexr. White, representative from Virginia, communicated his apprehensions that a disposition prevailed among the Eastern & Northern States, (discoverable from many circumstances, as well as from some late expressions which had fallen from some of their members in the Ho.) to pay little attention to the Western Country because they were of opinion it would soon shake off its dependence on this,[72] and in the meantime would be burthensome to it.

He gave some information also of the temper of the Western Settlers, of their dissatisfactions, and among other things that few of the Magistrates had taken the oath to the New Government, not inclining in the present state of things and under their ideas of neglect to bind themselves to it by an oath.

Sunday, 2d.

Went to Trinity Church in the forenoon—writing letters on private business in the afternoon—among other letters one by my order to Genl. Moylan,[73] to know if he wd. ac-

---

[72] The settlers west of the Alleghanies became very restless because of the delay in the negotiations for the free navigation of the Mississippi; and in the summer of 1794, very serious movements, of a seditious character, were made in Kentucky, which at one time threatened a separation of a portion at least of the Western territory of the Union. Menaces of this kind were heard from time to time, until the failure of Burr's scheme in 1806.

[73] Stephen Moylan, a colonel in the continental army during a portion of the Revolution.

cept the Consulate at Lisbon, as it was not proposed to give Salaries therewith.

MONDAY, 3d.

Exercised on Horseback about 9 o'clock.

After my return, the Secretary of the Treasury called upon me, and informed me that by some conversation he had had with Mr. King, (of the Senate) it appeared that there was a probability the Senate would take up the Sales by the Legislature of Georgia, and the affairs of the Indians which would be involved therein in a serious manner; and gave it as his opinion that if this was likely to be the case, it might be better for me to let the matter originate there, than with the Executive.

The Secretary of State furnished me with his opinion on these subjects—see his Statement—the substance of it is, that the State of Georgia by having adopted the Constitution, relinquished their right to treat with, or to regulate any matters with the Indians who were not subject thereto —consequently could not delegate a power they did not possess to others and that there was good & strong ground on which to contend this matter—but inasmuch as there was a party in the State opposed to the Sales before mentioned, but which might unite to defeat a Proclamation if one should be issued upon the Plan of the Secretary at War, he suggested the propriety of a representation to the State in the first instance for the purpose of undoing in a manner least hurtful to the feelings of it, the impolitic act of the Legislature—& in the meantime—at the meeting proposed to be held by the Indians in the Month of June ensuing to make these people perfectly sensible of the Sentiments and intentions of the general Government towards them.

TUESDAY, 4th.

Exercised in the forenoon on Horseback.
A respectable Company at the Levee to-day.

WEDNESDAY, 5th.

Requested General Rufus Putnam—lately appointed a Judge in the Western Government—and who was on the eve of his departure for that Country[74] to give me the best discription he could obtain of the proximity of the Waters of the Ohio and Lake Erie—the nature of their navigations —Portages,—&c.—also of the occurrences in the Country —the population of it—Temper of the people, &c. &c.

THURSDAY, 6th.

Exercised on horseback in the forenoon.—The following, out of several others who were invited, but prevented by

---

74 Putnam was an active officer in the engineer's department throughout the whole war for Independence. He was commissioned a brigadier in the continental army in 1783, when, on account of returning peace, he left military life, and engaged in the formation of a company for emigrating to and settling in the Ohio country. Thither he went in the spring of 1788, as the general agent, accompanied by about forty settlers, and pitching their tents at the mouth of the Muskingum River, planted the seed of a great commonwealth, and called the settlement Marietta. Washington appointed him Judge of the Supreme Court of the Northwest Territory in 1789.

sickness, dined here—viz.—Mr. Wingate, Mr. Maclay, Mr. Walker (of the Senate)—and Messrs. Gilman, Aimes, Genl. Muhlenburg, Wynkoop, Page and Lady, Smith So. Carolina & Lady, and Mr. White & his Lady of the House of Representatives.

Friday, 7th.

Exercised in the forenoon—Endeavoured through various channels to ascertain what places required, and the characters fittest for Consuls at them.

As the House of Representatives had reduced the Sum, in a Bill to provide for the expences of characters in the diplomatic line, below what would enable the Executive to employ the number which the exigencies of Government might make necessary, I thought it proper to intimate to a member or two of the Senate the places that were in contemplation to send persons to in this line—viz to France & England (when the latter manifested a disposition to treat us with more respect than she had done upon a former occasion) Ministers Plenipotentiary — and to Spain, Portugal & Holland Chargé des Affaires, and having an opportunity, mentioned the matter unofficially both to Mr. Carroll & Mr. Izard.

Much Company—Gentlemen & Ladies—visited Mrs. Washington this Evening.

Saturday, 8th.

Exercised in the Coach with Mrs. Washington & the Children in the forenoon.

Received from Genl. Knox, Secretary Genl. of the

triennial Genl. Meeting of the Cincinnati held at Philadelphia the first Monday of this Month, the Copy of an
Address from that body to me to which I was to return an
answer on ——— next.

SUNDAY, 9th.

Indisposed with a bad cold, and at home all day writing
letters on private business.

A severe illness with which I was siezed the 10th of this
month and which left me in a convalescent state for several
weeks after the violence of it had passed; & little inclination to do more than what duty to the public required at
my hands occasioned the suspension of this Diary.[75]

JUNE, 1790.

THURSDAY, 24th.

Exercised on horseback betwn. 5 & 7 o'clock, P. M.
Entertained the following Gentlemen at Dinner—viz—

---

[75] Incessant application to business made severe inroads upon Washington's health; and on the tenth of May, he was seized with a " severe
illness," as he remarks, which reduced him to the verge of dissolution.
He was confined to his chamber for several weeks. His chief difficulty
was inflammation of the lungs; and he suffered from general debility
until the close of the session of Congress, in August. Then, accompanied by Jefferson, he made a voyage to Newport, Rhode Island, for the
benefit of his health, and incidentally to have personal intercourse with
the leading inhabitants there, he having avoided Rhode Island, in his
recent Eastern tour, for reasons explained in note 27, on page 52. The
sea-voyage was beneficial to his health, and soon after his return, at the
close of August, he set out with his family, for Mount Vernon.

Messrs. Gerry, Goodhue, Grout, Leonard, Huntingdon, Benson, Boudinot, Cadwalader, Sinnichson, Heister, Scott, Contee, Stone, Brown, and Morse of the House of Representatives.

Received from the Committee of Enrollment the Act for extending the Judiciary Law to the State of Rhode Island & Providence Planns.

FRIDAY, 25th.

Constant & heavy Rain all day, prevented Company from visiting Mrs. Washington this afternoon & all kinds of Exercise.

SATURDAY, 26th.

Exercised in the Coach with Mrs. Washington & the Children & by walking in the afternoon.

SUNDAY, 27th.

Went to Trinity Church in the forenoon—and employed myself in writing business in the afternoon.

MONDAY, 28th.

Exercised between 5 & 7 o'clock in the morning & drank Tea with Mrs. Clinton (the Governors Lady) in the afternoon.

TUESDAY, 29th.

Exercised between 5 & 7 o'clock in the morning on horseback.

A good deal of Company, amongst which several strangers and some foreigners at the Levee to day.

On consultation with the Secretary of State to day, it
was thought advisable to direct him to provide two
Medals, one for the Marqs. de la Luzerne, formerly Minister Plenipo. from France to the U. States of America, &
the other for Mr. Van Berkel late Minister from Holland;
& to have the Dies with which they were to be struck in
France, sent over here.—The cost of these Medals would
be about 30 Guineas; but the Chain for that designed for
the Marqs. de la Luzerne (on acct. of his attachment &
Services to this Country) was directed to Cost about 200
Guineas—the other about 100 Guins.

WEDNESDAY, 30th.

Recd. from the Committee of Enrollment the following
Acts.—viz.—" An Act providing the means of intercourse
between the United States and foreign Nations." By
which the President of the United States is authorized to
draw from the Treasury 40,000 dollars annually, for the
support of such persons as he shall Commission to serve
the U. States in foreign pts. and for the expence incident
to the business in which they may be employed.—Not
more than 9000 Dollars to be allowed to a Minister Plenipotentiary, nor 4500 to a Chargé des Affaires, except the
outfit to each, which shall not exceed one years salary;—
nor shall more than 1300 dollars be allowed to the Secretary of any Minister Plenipotentiary.—The President is to
acct. specifically for all such Expenditures as in his judg-

ment may be made public—and also for the amount of such Expenditures, as he may think it advisable not to specify, and cause a regular statement thereof to be laid before Congress annually.

" An Act, for the Relief of Nathaniel Twining" and " An Act to satisfy the Claims of John Mc. Cord against the United States." These several Acts were presented to me about 10 o'clock A. M.

THURSDAY.

J U L Y 1st.

Exercised between 5 and 7 o'clock on Horseback.

Announced to the House of Representatives (where the Bills originated) that my signature had been given to the Acts above mentioned.

Having put into the hands of the Vice President of the U. States the Communications of Mr. Gouvr. Morris, who had been empowered to make informal enquiries how well disposed the British Ministry might be to enter into Commercial regulations with the United States, and to fulfil the Articles of Peace respecting our Western Posts, and the Slaves which had been carried from this Country,[76]

---

[76] At the beginning of this year, a general European war appeared inevitable. A long-pending controversy between Spain and Great Britain remained unsettled. It was believed that France would espouse the cause of Spain ; and it was thought a favorable moment for the United States to press upon Great Britain the fulfilment, on her part, of the treaty of 1783, concerning the matters to which Washington here alludes. There was then no diplomatic intercourse between

he expressed his approbation that this step had been taken; and added that the disinclination of the British Cabinet to comply with the two latter, & to evade the former, as evidently appears from the Correspondence of Mr. Morris with the Duke of Leeds (the British Minister for Foreign affairs) was of a piece with their conduct towds. him whilst Minister at that Court; & just what he expected;—& that to have it ascertained was necessary.

He thought, as a rupture betwn. England & Spain was almost inevitable, that it would be our policy & interest to take part with the latter as he was very apprehensive that New Orleans was an object with the former; their possessing which would be very injurious to us;—but he observed, at the same time, that the situation of our affairs would not justify the measure unless the People themselves (of the United States) should take the lead in the business.

Received about three o'clock, official information from Colo. Willet, that he was on the return from the Creek Nation (whither he had been sent with design to bring Colo. Mc. Gillivray, and some of the Chiefs of these people to the City of New York for the purpose of treating,) that he with the said Mc. Gillivray and many of the head men, were advanced as far as Hopewell in So. Carolina on their way hither—and that they should proceed by the way of Richmond with as much expedition as the nature of the case wd. admit.

---

the two governments; and Gouverneur Morris, who had been some time in Paris, was commissioned by Washington as a special agent to open a communication upon the subject with the British minister for foreign affairs.

It having been reported upon information being received at St. Augustine of Col°· Mc. Gillivrays intention of coming to this place that advice thereof was immediately forwarded by the Commandant of the place to the Governor of the Havanah—And a Mr. Howard Secretary of East Florida and an influential character there, and on pretext of bad health, and a Spanish Armed Brig of 20 Guns, ostensibly to bring 50,000 dollars for the purpose of buying Flour, arriving here immediately thereupon, affording strong ground to suspect that the money & the character above mentioned, were sent here for the purpose of Counteracting the Negotiations which was proposed to be held with Col°· Mc. Gillivray & the other Chiefs of the Creeks—& this suspicion being corroberated by Mr. Howard's visit to Philadelphia, I directed the Secretary at War to advertise Col°· Willet thereof—that he might, if a meeting should take place at Philadelphia, or elsewhere on the Rd. observe their conduct & penetrate if possible into the object of it. He was desired at the same time to make suitable provision for lodging, & otherwise entertaining Col°· Mc. Gillivray & his party.

The following Gentn. & Ladies dined here to day—viz— The Secretary of State, Secretary of the Treasury, and Secretary at War & their Ladies—Mr. Dalton & Mr. King & their Ladies, Mr. Butler & his two daughters—Mr. Hawkins, Mr. Stanton, & Mr. Foster, & Mr. Izard.—The Chief Justice & his Lady, Genl. Schuyler & Mrs. Izard, were also invited but were otherwise engaged.

FRIDAY, 2nd.

Exercised between 5 & 7 on horseback.

About one o'clock, official accounts of the safety of
Major Doughty (who was sent on important business to the
Chickasaw and Choctaw Nations of Indians) were received ; together with the detail of his proceedings to the
Country of the former, and the misfortune that attended
him in ascending the River Tenessee. to the intended place
of meeting the Chicasaws, by the Treachery of a Banditti
composed of Cherokees, Shawanese & Creek Indians who
to the number of 40 in 4 canoes (Doughty's party consisting of no more than 15 Soldiers) under colour of a white
flag, & professions of friendship rose, fired upon, & killed
five & wounded six more of his men ; obliging him (when
within six miles of Ochappo the place of the Rendezvous,)
to Retreat down the Tennessee & which he was able to
effect by his gallant behaviour & good conduct ; notwithstanding the superior force of the enemy & a pursuit of
4 hours and attemps to board the Barge in wch. he was.—
But being too weak to ascend the Ohio after he had
entered it, he was induced to follow the Currnt. into the
Missisippi & thence down the same to a Spanish post, A
—— de Grass about —— miles below the Mouth of the
Ohio where he was treated with great kindness & civility
by Monsr. —— the Commandant.—He contrived after
this to see the Piemingo & other head Men of the Chic-
asaw Nation with whom he did the business he was sent
on nearly as well as if he had got to Occhappo the place of

his destination as will appear by his details transmitted to the Secretary at War.

Received from the Committee of Enrollment two Acts.— One "For giving effect to an Act entitled "An Act providing for the enumeration of the Inhabitants of the United States," "in respect to *to* the State of Rhode Island & Providence Plantations,"—The other, "An Act to authorize the purchase of a tract of Land for the use of the United States.

Much company of both Sexes to visit Mrs. Washington this evening.

SATURDAY, 3d.

Exercised between 9 and 11 in the Coach with Mrs. Washington and the Children.

The policy of treating Col°· Mc. Gillivray, & the Chiefs of the Creek Nation who were coming with him, with attention as they passed through the States to this City induced me to desire the Secretary at War to write to the Governors of Virginia, Maryland & Pensylvania requesting that they might be provided at the expence with whatever might be deemed a proper respect that they might be kept in good humour.

Nominated, *Yesterday*, to the Senate, persons for the Judiciary of Rhode Island; and a person as Naval Officer in the District of Providence, in the place of Mr. Foster, who was sent by the State as one of their Senators—also Surveyors for the smaller Ports in the District & the District of New-Port.

SUNDAY, 4th.

Went to Trinity Church in the forenoon.

This day being the Anniversary of The declaration of Independency the celebration of it was put of until to morrow.

MONDAY, 5th.

The members of the Senate, House of Representatives, Public Officers, Foreign Characters &c. The Members of the Cincinnati, Officers of the Militia, &c., came with the compliments of the day to me——about one o'clock a sensible Oration was delivered in St. Pauls Chapel by Mr. Brockholst Levingston,[77] on the occasion of the day—the tendency of which was, to show the different situation we are now in, under an excellent government of our own choice, to what it would have been if we had not succeeded in our opposition to the attemps of Great Britain to enslave us ; and how much we ought to cherish the blessings which are within our reach, & to cultivate the seeds of harmony & unanimity in all our public Councils.—There were several other points touched upon in sensible manner.

In the afternoon many Gentlemen & ladies visited Mrs. Washington.

---

[77] Son of William Livingston, who had been governor of New Jersey. Mr. Livingston was afterwards a leader of the Republican party, in opposition to Jay's treaty with Great Britain, negotiated at the close of 1794. Mr. Jay was his brother-in-law, and Mr. Livingston had accompanied that gentleman in his mission to Spain, as private secretary, in 1779. In 1802, he was appointed Judge of the Supreme Court of the United States, and died in 1823.

I was informed this day by General Irvine (who recd. the acct. from Pittsburgh,) that the Traitor Arnold was at Detroit & had viewed the Militia in the Neighbourhood of it twice.—This had occasioned much Speculation in those parts—and with many other circumstances—though trifling in themselves led strongly to a conjecture that the British had some design on the Spanish settlements on the Mississipi and of course to surround these United States.

Tuesday, 6th.

Exercised on Horseback betwn. 5 & 7 o'clock in the morning,—at 9 o'clock I sat for Mr. Trumbull to finish my pictures in some of his historical pieces.

Anounced to the House of Representatives (where the Bills originated) my Assent to the Acts which were presented to me on Friday last.—One of which Authorizes the President to purchase the whole, or such part of that tract of Land situate in the State of New York, commonly called West-point as shall be by him judged requisite for the purpose of such fortifications & Garrisons as may be necessary for the defence of the same.

The visitors were few to day, on acct. of the numbers that paid their compliments yesterday.

Wednesday, 7th.

Exercised between 5 & 7 this morning on Horseback.

Thursday, 8th.

Sat from 9 o'clock till after 10 for Mr. Jno. Trumbull,

who was drawing a Portrait of me at full length which he intended to present to Mrs. Washington.

About noon the Secret..ies of State, and of the Treasury called upon me—the last of whom reported a communication made to him by Majr. Beckwith Aid de camp to Lord Dorchester—Governor of Canada,[18] wch. he reduced to writing, and is as follows.

" Memorandum of the substance of a communication "made on Thursday the eighth day of July 1790 to " the Subscriber by Major Beckwith as by direction of " Lord Dorchester."

" Major Beckwith began by stating that Lord Dorches- " ter had directed him to make his acknowledgmts. for the " politeness which had been shown in respect to the desire " he had intimated to pass by N. York in his way to Eng- " land ; adding that the prospect of a War between Great " Britain & Spain would prevent or defer the execution of " his intention in that particular."

" He next proceeded to observe that Lord Dorchester "had been informed of a negotiation commenced on the " other side of the Water through the agency of Mr. Mor- " ris ; mentioning as the subscriber understood principally " by way of proof of Lord Dorchester's knowledge of the " transaction that Mr. Morris had not produced any regular

---

[18] Lord Dorchester (Sir Guy Carleton) had asked leave to pass through New York, on his way to England. Permission was readily granted.   Under a pretext of making a formal acknowledgment for the consent, he dispatched Major Beckwith to New York, with the real design of sounding the United States government concerning its disposition towards England and France.

" Credentials, but merely a letter from the President di-
" rected to himself, that some delays had intervened partly
" on account of Mr. Morris's absence on a trip to Holland
" as was understood and that it was not improbable these
" delays & some other circumstances may have impressed
" Mr. Morris with an idea of backwardness on the part of
" the British Ministry."

" That his Lordship however had directed him to say
" that an inference of this sort would not in his opinion be
" well founded as he had reason to believe that the Cabinet
" of Great Britain entertained a disposition not only to-
" wards a friendly intercourse but towards an alliance with
" the United States.

" Major Beckwith then proceeded to speak of the partic-
" ular cause of the expected rupture between Spain & Brit-
" ain observing it was one in which all Commercial Nations
" must be supposed to favor the views of G. Britain.—That
" it was therefore presumed, should a war take place, that
" the United States would find it to be their interest to
" take part with G. Britain rather than with Spain."

" Major Beckwith afterwards mentioned that Lord Dor-
" chester had heard with great concern of some depreda-
" tions committed by some Indians on our Western frontier.
" That he wished it to be believed that nothing of this kind
" had received the least countenance from him.—That on
" the contrary he had taken every proper opportunity of in-
" culcating upon the Indians a pacific disposition towards
" us ; and that as soon as he had heard of the outrages
" lately committed he had sent a message to endeavor to
" prevent them.—That his Lordship had understd. that the

"Indians alluded to were a banditti composed chiefly or in
"great part of Creeks or Cherokees, over whom he had no
"influence; intimating at the same time that these tribes
"were supposed to be in connection with the Spaniards."

"He stated in the next place that his Lordship had been
"informed that a Captain Hart in our Service and a Mr.
"Wemble, and indeed, some persons in the Treaty at Fort
"Harmer had thrown out menaces with regard to the posts
"on the Frontier & had otherwise held very intemperate
"language; which however his Lordship considered rather
"as effusions of individual feelings than as effects of any
"instruction from authority."

"Major Beckwith concluded with producing a letter
"signed Dorchester; which letter contained ideas simalar
"to those he had expressed, though in more guarded terms
"and without any allusions to instructions from the British
"Cabinet.—This letter it is recollected hints at the non-
"execution of the treaty of peace on our part."

"On the subscriber remarking the circumstance that this
"letter seemed to speak only the Sentiments of his Lord-
"ship, Major Beckwith replied that whatever reasons there
"might be for that course of proceeding in the present Stage
"of the business, it was to be presumed that his Lordship
"knew too well the consequence of such a step to have
"taken it without a previous knowledge of the intentions
"of the Cabinet."

The aspect of this business in the moment of its com-
munication to me, appeared simply, and no other than this;
—We did not incline to give any satisfactory answer to
Mr. Morris, who was *officially* commissioned to ascertain our

intentions with respect to the evacuation of the Western Posts within the territory of the United States and other matters into which he was empowered to enquire until by this unauthenticated mode we can discover whether you will enter into an alliance with us and make Common cause against Spain.—In that case we will enter into a Commercial Treaty with you & *promise perhaps* to fulfil what they already stand engaged to perform—However, I requested Mr. Jefferson & Col$^{o.}$ Hamilton, as I intend to do the Vice President, Chief Justice & Secretary at War, to revolve this matter in all its relations in their minds that they may be the better prepared to give me their opinions thereon in the course of 2 or three days.

The following Gentlemen dined here to day—viz— Messrs. Wingate, Strong, Mc. Clay, Lee, & Johnson (No. Carolina) of the Senate — and Messrs. Gilman, Aimes, Sturges, Schureman, Fitzsimmons, Wynkoop, Vining, Smith, Madison, Sevier, & Sumpter, of the House of Representatives.

FRIDAY, 9th.

Exercised on Horseback between 5 & 7 in the morning.

A letter from Genl. Harmer,[79] enclosing copies of former letters; and Sundry other papers, were put into my hands by the Secretary at War.—By these it appears that the frequent hostilities of some vagabond Indians, who it was supposed had a mind to establish themselves on the Sciota

---

[79] General Harmar was in command of United States troops in the Northwest Territory.

for the purpose of robbing the Boats, and murdering the Passengers in their descent or assent of the Ohio, had induced an Expedition composed of 120 effective men of the Regular Troops under his (Harmer's) command, and 202 Militia, (mounted on Horses) under that of Genl. Scott of the District of Kentucky.—This force rendezvoused at the mouth of Lime-stone on the 20 of April; and intended by a detour to fall on the Scioto high up;—five miles above the mouth of Paint Creek (which runs through the finest land in the world, & surveyed for the Officers of the Virginia line) it accordingly struck the Scioto on the 25th 50 miles from its mouth. But the Militia, according to custom, getting tired, & short of Provisions, became clamorous to get home; & many of them would have gone off but for the influence of Genl. Scott; however, the March was continued and on the 27th the Troops arrived at the mouth of the Scioto where crossing the Ohio the Militia seperated for their respective homes & the Regular Troops proceeded up to their head Quarters at Fort Washington[80] —In this expedition little was done;—a small party of 4 Indians was discovered—killed & scalped—and at another place some Bever traps & skins were taken at an Indian Camp—the detour made was about 128 miles & had the Militia crossed to the East side of the Scioto it is supposed several parties of Indians would have been fallen in with,— the Scioto is 65 miles below the mouth of Licking.

Among the Enclosures with Genl. Harmer's letter, were Captn. Hart's Report of the Navigations of Big-beaver and

---

[80] On the site of Cincinnati.

the Cayahoga, and Country between; and of other waters : —also Majr. Hamtramck's report of the distances &c. from Post Vincennes on the Wabash to Detroit—copies of which I desired to be furnished with.

Many visitors (male & female) this afternoon to Mrs. Washington.

SATURDAY, 10th.

Having formed a Party, consisting of the Vice President, his lady, Son & Miss Smith; the Secretaries of State, Treasury, & War, and the ladies of the two latter; with all the Gentlemen of my family, Mrs. Lear [81] & the two Children, we visited the old position of Fort Washington and afterwards dined on a dinner provided by Mr. Mariner [82] at the House lately Col⁰· Roger Morris, but confiscated and in the occupation of a common Farmer. [83]

---

[81] Wife of Tobias Lear, Washington's private secretary. She was a young and beautiful lady. Judge Iredell, of North Carolina, in a letter to his wife, written at Philadelphia, in July, 1793, said: " We have lately had a very affecting death in this city. Mrs. Lear, the wife of Mr. Lear, the President's secretary, died on Sunday last after a short but very severe illness. She was only 23, and beloved and respected by all who knew her ; and she and her husband had been fond of each other from infancy. He attended the funeral himself, and so did the President and Mrs. Washington. Mr. Hamilton, Mr. Jefferson, General Knox, Judge Wilson, Judge Peters and myself were pall-bearers."

[82] See note 10, on page 18.

[83] The mansion is yet standing upon the high bank of the Harlem river, at 169th Street, a little below the High Bridge of the Croton aqueduct. It is the property of Madame Jumel, widow of Aaron Burr. Its situation is one of the most picturesque on the island, commanding a fine view of the surrounding country, with the great city and clustering villages. It is about a mile from the site of old Fort Washing-

I requested the Vice President & the Secretary at War as I had also in the Morning the Chief Justice, to turn their attention to the communications of Majr. Beckwith : as I might, in course of a few days, call for their opinions on the important matter of it.

SUNDAY, 11th.

At home all day—dispatching some business relative to my own private concerns.

MONDAY, 12th.

Exercised on Horseback between 5 & 6 in the morning.

Sat for Mr. Trumbull from 9 until half after ten.—And about Noon had two Bills presented to me by the joint Committee of Congress—The one " An Act for Establishing the Temporary & permanent Seat of the Government of the United States." The other "An Act further to provide for the payment of the Invalid Pensioners of the United States."

TUESDAY, 13th.

Again sat for Mr. Trumbull from 9 until half past 10 o'clock.

A good deal of Company at the Levee to day.

---

ton. Colonel Roger Morris was Washington's companion in arms at the defeat of Braddock, and his successful rival in claims for the hand of Mary Phillipse, in 1756. Morris was a Loyalist, and fled, with his family, to the Hudson Highlands, when the Revolution broke out. Washington occupied this house as his quarters a short time in 1776, when the American army lay on Harlem Heights.

WEDNESDAY, 14th.

Exercised on Horseback from 5 until near 7 o'clock.

Had some further conversation to day with the Chief Justice and Secretary of the Treasury with respect to the business on which Majr. Beckwith was come on.—The result—To treat his communications very civilly—to intimate, delicately, that they carried no marks official or authentic, nor in speaking of Alliance, did they convey any definite meaning by which the precise object of the British Cabinet could be discovered.—In a word, that the Secretary of the Treasury was to extract as much as he could from Major Beckwith and to report to me, without committing, by any assurances whatever, the Government of the U. States, leaving it entirely free to pursue, unreproached, such a line of conduct in the dispute as her interest (& honour) shall dictate.

MARCH—21st—1791.

MONDAY.

Left Philadelphia about 11 o'clock to make a tour through the Southern States.[84]—Reached Chester about 3 o'clock—dined & lodged at Mr. Wythes—Roads exceedingly deep, heavy & cut in places by the Carriages which used them.

In this tour I was accompanied by Majr. Jackson,—my equipage & attendance consisted of a Charriot & four horses drove in hand—a light baggage Waggon & two horses—four saddle horses besides a led one for myself—and five—to wit—my Valet de Chambre, two footmen, Coachman & postilion.

TUESDAY, 22d.

At half past 6 o'clock we left Chester, & breakfasted at Wilmington.—Finding the Roads very heavy—and receiving unfavourable Accts. of those between this place and Baltimore, I determined to cross the Bay by the way of Rockhall—and crossing Christiana Creek proceeded through Newcastle & by the Red Lyon to the Buck tavern 13 miles

---

[84] He and his family left his residence in Market-street, Philadelphia, in his English coach, at twelve o'clock this day. They were accompanied as far as Delaware by Mr. Jefferson and General Knox, two of the heads of departments. Also by Major Jackson, his aid, who accompanied him in his entire journey through the Southern States.

from Newcastle and 19 from Wilmington where we dined
and lodged.—At the Red Lyon we gave the horses a bite
of Hay—during their eating of which I discovered that one
of those wch. drew the Baggage waggon was lame and
apprd. otherwise much indisposed—had him bled and afterwards led to the Buck-tavern.

This is a better house than the appearances indicate.

WEDNESDAY, 23d.

Set off at 6 o'clock—breakfasted at Warwick—bated
with hay 9 miles farther—and dined and lodged at the
House of one Worrell's in Chester; from whence—I sent
an Express to Rock Hall[85] to have Boats ready for me by
9 o'clock to morrow morning—after doing which Captn.
Nicholson obligingly set out for that place to see that
every thing should prepared against my arrival.

The lame horse was brought on, and while on the Road
apprd. to move tolerably well, but as soon as he stopped,
discovered a stiffness in all his limbs, which indicated some
painful disorder—I fear a Chest founder.—My riding horse
also appeared to be very unwell, his appetite had entirely
failed him.

The Winter grain along the Road appeared promising
and abundant.

THURSDAY, 24th.

Left Chestertown about 6 o'clock—before nine I arrived

---

[85] In Kent county, Maryland, nearly seventy miles Northeast from
Annapolis.

at Rock-Hall where we breakfasted and immediately; after which we began to embark—The doing of which employed us (for want of contrivance) until near 3 o'clock,—and then one of my Servants (Paris) & two horses were left, notwithstanding two Boats in aid of the two Ferry Boats were procured.—Unluckily, embarking on board of a borrowed Boat because she was the largest, I was in imminent danger, from the unskillfulness of the hands, and the dulness of her sailing, added to the darkness and storminess of the night—for two hours after we hoisted sail the wind was light and ahead—the next hour was a start calm—after which the wind sprung up at So. Et. and increased until it blew a gale—about which time, and after 8 o'clock P. M. we made the Mouth of Severn River (leading up to Annapolis) but the ignorance of the People on board, with respect to the navigation of it run us a ground first on Greenbury point from whence with much exertion and difficulty we got off; & then, having no knowledge of the Channel and the night being immensely dark with heavy and variable squals of wind—constant lightning & tremendous thunder—we soon got aground again on what is called Horne's point—where finding all efforts in vain, & not knowing where we were we remained, not knowing what might happen, till morning.

Friday, 25th.

Having lain all night in my Great Coat & Boots, in a birth not long enough for me by the head, & much cramped; we found ourselves in the morning within about one mile of Annapolis, & still fast aground.—Whilst we were preparing our small Boat in order to land in it, a sailing Boat came of to our assistance in wch. with the Baggage I had on board I landed, & requested Mr. Man at whose Inn I intended lodging, to send off a Boat to take off two of my Horses & Chariot which I had left on board and with it my Coachman to see that it was properly done—but by mistake the latter not having notice of this order & attempting to get on board afterwards in a small sailing Boat was overset and narrowly escaped drowning.

Was informed upon my arrival (when 15 Guns were fired) that all my other horses arrived safe that embarked at the same time I did, about 8 o'clock last night.

Was waited upon by the Governor (who came off in a Boat as soon as he heard I was on my passage from Rock-Hall to meet us, but turned back when it grew dark and squally) as soon as I arrived at Man's tavern & was engaged by him to dine with the Citizens of Annapolis this day at Mann's tavern, and at his House to morrow— the first I accordingly did.

Before dinner I walked with him, and several other Gentlemen to the State house,[86] (which seems to be much out of repair)—the College of St. John at which there are about 80 Students of every description, and then by way of the Governor's (to see Mrs. Howell) home.

---

[86] This venerable building is yet standing. There the Continental Congress assembled in December, 1783, to receive from Washington his commission as Commander-in-chief, which he resigned into their hands.

SATURDAY, 26th.

Spent the forenoon in my Room preparing papers &c. against my arrival at George-Town.

Dined at the Governors—and went to the Assembly in the Evening where I stayed till half past ten o'clock.

In the afternoon of this day Paris and my other two horses arrived from Rock-Hall.

SUNDAY, 27th.

About 9 o'clock this morning I left Annapolis, under a discharge of Artillery, and being accompanied by the Governor a Mr. Kilty of the Council and Mr. Charles Stuart proceeded on my Journey for George-Town. Bated at Queen Ann,[87] 13 miles distant and dined and lodged at Bladensburgh.[88]—Many of the Gentlemen of Annapolis, (among was the Chancellor of the State) escorted me to the ferry over So. River.

MONDAY, 28th.

Left Bladensburgh at half after six, & breakfasted at George Town about 8;[89] where, having appointed the

---

[87] Queen Anne, on the Patuxent, on the road from Annapolis to Washington City, was then quite a flourishing village. It is now in decay.

[88] Four miles from Washington City. This place is famous on account of a battle fought there between the American and British in 1814; also as the place where Commodore Decatur was mortally wounded in a duel with Commodore Barron.

[89] The site of Washington City was then a half-uncultivated wilder-

Commissioners under the Residence Law to meet me, I found Mr. Johnson one of them[90] (& who is Chief Justice of the State) in waiting—& soon after came in David Stuart,[91] & Danl. Carroll[92] Esqrs. the other two.—A few miles out of Town I was met by the principal Citizens of the place and escorted in by them; and dined at Suter's tavern (where I also lodged) at a public dinner given by the Mayor & Corporation—previous to which I examined the Surveys of Mr. Ellicot[93] who had been sent on to lay out the district of ten miles square for the federal seat; and also the works of Majr. L'Enfant who had been engaged to examine & make a draught of the grds. in the vicinity of George Town and Carrollsburg on the Eastern branch making arrangements for examining the ground myself to morrow with the Commissioners.

---

ness, the commissioners appointed for the purpose not having completed their surveys. Pennsylvania Avenue is upon a line of a path which then passed through an alder swamp, from the high ground on which the President's house stands, to the Capitoline Hill.

[90] Thomas Johnson, who was the first republican governor of Maryland, from 1777 to 1779.

[91] Dr. David Stuart married the widow of John Parke Custis, the son of Mrs. Washington. These commissioners were appointed under the "Residence Law," so called because it was enacted for the purpose of fixing the permanent residence of the government.

[92] Daniel Carroll, brother apparently of the Most Rev. John Carroll, archbishop of Baltimore, was a representative in Congress from 1789 to 1791.

[93] Andrew Ellicott succeeded Major L'Enfant, in 1792, as engineer-in-chief in laying out the Federal City. L'Enfant had served as an engineer in the Continental army during a part of the Revolution.

TUESDAY, 29th.

In a thick mist, and under strong appearances of a
settled rain (which however did not happen) I set out
about 7 o'clock, for the purpose above mentioned—but
from the unfavorableness of the day, I derived no great
satisfaction from the review.

Finding the interests of the Landholders about George
town and those about Carrollsburgh much at varience and
that their fears and jealousies of each were counteracting
the public purposes & might prove injurious to its best
interests whilst if properly managed they might be made to
subserve it—I requested them to meet me at six o'clock
this afternoon at my lodgings, which they accordingly did.

To this meeting I represented that the contention in
which they seemed engaged, did not in my opinion comport either with the public interest or that of their own ;—
that while each party was aiming to obtain the public
buildings, they might by placing the matter on a contract-
ed scale, defeat the measure altogether; not only by pro-
crastination but for want of the means necessary to effect
the work ;—That niether the offer from George-town or
Carrollsburgh, seperately, was adequate to the end of
insuring the object.—That both together did not compre-
hend more ground nor would afford greater means than
was required for the federal City ;—and that, instead of
contending which of the two should have it they had
better, by combining more offers make a common cause of
it, and thereby secure it to the district——other arguments
were used to show the danger which might result from

delay and the good effects that might proceed from a Union.

Dined at Col⁰· Forrest's to day with the Commissioners & others.

Wednesday, 30th.

The parties to whom I addressed myself yesterday evening, having taken the matter into consideration saw the propriety of my observations; and that whilst they were contending for the shadow they might loose the substance; and therefore mutually agreed and entered into articles to surrender for public purposes, one half of the land they severally possessed within bounds which were designated as necessary for the City to stand with some other stipulations, which were inserted in the instrument which they respectively subscribed.

This business being thus happily finished & some directions given to the Commissioners, the Surveyor and Engineer with respect to the mode of laying out the district—Surveying the grounds for the City & forming them into lots—I left Georgetown—dined in Alexandria & reached Mount Vernon in the evening.

Thursday, 31st.

From this time, until the 7th of April, I remained at Mount Vernon—visiting my Plantations every day.—and

Was obliged also, consequence of Col⁰· Henry Lee's declining to accept the command of one of the Regiments of Levies and the request of the Secretary at War to appoint those officers which had been left to Col⁰· Lee to

do for a Battalion to be raised in Virginia East of the
Alligany Mountains to delay my journey on this account—
and after all, to commit the business as will appear by the
letters & for the reasons there mentioned to Col[o.] Darke's
management.[94]

From hence I also wrote letters to the Secretaries of
State,—Treasury,—and War, in answer to those received
from on interesting subjects—desiring in case of important
occurances they would hold a consultation and if they were
of such a nature as to make my return necessary to give
me notice & I would return immediately—My Rout was
given to them & the time I should be at the particular
places therein mentioned.[95]

THURSDAY, 7.—APRIL.

Recommenced my journey with Horses apparently much
refreshed and in good spirits.

In attempting to cross the ferry at Colchester with the
four Horses hitched to the Chariot by the neglect of the
person who stood before them, one of the leaders got overboard when the boat was in swimming water and 50 yards
from the shore—with much difficulty he escaped drowning

---

[94] Col. Darke was an active officer in the Ohio country, in the Indian
Wars in that region from 1792 to 1794 ; and Darke County was named
in his honor. He was with the Virginians at Braddock's defeat; was
in the war for Independence ; was a member of the Virginia Convention in 1788 ; was with St. Clair in his unfortunate campaign in 1791 ;
and died in 1801.

[95] See Washington's letter to the Heads of Departments, April 4,
1791, in Sparks' Life, &c., &c., 157.

before he could be disengaged—His struggling frightened the others in such a manner that one after another and in quick succession they all got overboard harnessed & fastened as they were and with the utmost difficulty they were saved & the Carriage escaped been dragged after them, as the whole of it happened in swimming water & at a distance from the shore—Providentially—indeed miraculously—by the exertions of people who went off in Boats & jumped into the River as soon as the Batteau was forced into wading water—no damage was sustained by the horses, Carriage or harness.

Proceeded to Dumfries where I dined—after which I visited & drank Tea with my Niece Mrs. Thos. Lee.

FRIDAY, 8th.

Set out about 6 o'clock—breakfasted at Stafford Court House—and dined and lodged at my Sister Lewis's in Fredericksburgh.[96]

SATURDAY, 9th.

Dined at an entertained given by the Citizens of the town.—Received and answered an address from the Corporation.

Was informed by Mr. Jno. Lewis, who had, not long since been in Richmond, that Mr. Patrick Henry had

---

[96] His sister Elizabeth, married Colonel Fielding Lewis. His son, Lawrence Lewis, was Washington's favorite nephew. He married Nelly Custis, Mrs. Washington's grand-daughter, and resided with her at Mount Vernon at the time of Washington's death.

avowed his interest in the Yazoo Company ;[97] and made
him a tender of admission into it, whch. he declined—
but asking, if the Company did not expect the Settlement of the lands would be disagreeable to the Indians was
answered by Mr. Henry that the Co, intended to apply to
Congress for protection—which, if not granted they would
have recourse to their own means to protect the settlement
—That General Scott had a certain quantity of Land (I
think 40.000 acres in the Company's grant & was to have
the command of the force which was to make the establishment—and moreover—that General Muhlenburg had offered £1000 for a certain part of the grant—the quantity I do
not recollect if it was mentioned to me.

Sunday, 10th.

Left Fredericksburgh about 6 o'clock,—myself Majr. Jackson and one Servant breakfasted at General Spotswoods[98]

---

[97] The first legislature of Georgia, after the adoption of the Federal
Constitution, undertook to sell out, to three private companies, the
pre-emption right to vast tracts of land west of the Chattahoochee
river, unmindful of any rightful claim of the Indians. They were
called Yazoo Land Companies. They sold to the South Carolina Yazoo
Company 5,000,000 acres for $66,964 ; to the Virginia Yazoo Company
7,000,000 acres, for $93,742 ; and to the Tennessee Yazoo Company,
3,500,000 acres for $46,875. These companies not complying with the
requirements of the sale, a succeeding legislature declared the bargain
a nullity. Some of the purchasers contested the claims, and litigations
arose, which became still more complicated when the same lands were
sold to other companies.

[98] Alexander Spottswood, an officer in the continental army. He and
Washington were intimate friends, and frequently corresponded on
agricultural subjects.

—the rest of my Servants continued on to Todd's Ordinary where they also breakfasted.—Dined at the Bowling Green—and lodged at Kenner's Tavern 14 miles farther—in all 35 m.

MONDAY, 11th.

Took an early breakfast at Kinner's—bated at one Rawlings's half way between that & Richmd. and dined at the latter about 3 o'clock.—On my arrival was saluted by the Cannon of the place—waited on by the Governor[99] and other Gentlemen—and saw the City illuminated at night.

TUESDAY, 12th.

In company with the Governor,—The Directors of the James River Navigation Company[100]—the Manager & many other Gentlemen—I viewed the Canal, Sluces, Locks, & other works between the City of Richmond & Westham.—These together have brought the navigation to within a mile and half, or mile and $\frac{3}{4}$ of the proposed Bason; from which the Boats by means of Locks are to communicate with the tide water navigation below.—The Canal is of sufficient depth every where—but in places not brought to its proper width; it seems to be perfectly secure against Ice,

---

[99] Henry Lee. He was the son of Washington's first love—the "Lowland Beauty" of whom he was enamored when only sixteen years of age. Lee was the celebrated leader of the *Legion* in the Southern campaigns.

[100] Washington was president of this company. It had been formed several years before, for the purpose of promoting the internal commerce of the State.

Freshes & drift wood — The locks at the head of these works are simple—altogether of hewn stone, except the gates & cills — and very easy & convenient to work,— there are two of them, each calculated to raise and lower 6 feet—they cost according to the Manager's, Mr. Harris acct. about £3000 but I could see nothing in them to require such a sum to erect them.—The Sluces in the River, between the locks and the mouth of the Canal are well graduated and easy of assent—To complete the Canal from the point to which it is now opened, and the Locks at the foot of them, Mr. Harris thinks will require 3 years.

Received an Address from the Mayor, Aldermen & Common Council of the City of Richmond at three o'clock, & dined with the Governor at 4 o'clock.

In the course of my enquiries—chiefly from Col⁰· Carrington[101]—I cannot discover that any discontents prevail among the people at large, at the proceedings of Congress. —The conduct of the Assembly respecting the assumption[102] he thinks is condemned by them as intemperate & unwise—and he seems to have no doubt but that the Excise

---

[101] Colonel Edward Carrington, who was a meritorious officer in the campaigns in the South during the Revolution. He was now active as a United States marshal for a large district in Virginia.

[102] A part of Hamilton's financial scheme for the United States, was the assumption of the respective State debts by the general government. This gave rise to violent opposition, and was the chief cause of Jefferson's bitter hostility to Hamilton. Out of the party feelings engendered by the assumption scheme, grew the Republican party, that during the latter years of Washington's administration, gave him much trouble because of the unkind spirit of opposition to the measures of the government.

law—as it is called—may be executed without difficulty—
nay more, that it will become popular in a little time—His
duty as Marshall having carried him through all parts of
the State lately, and of course given him the best means of
ascertaining the temper & disposition of its Inhabitants—
he thinks them favorable towards the General Government
—& that they only require to have matters explained to
them in order to obtain their full assent to the measures
adopted by it.

WEDNESDAY, 13th.

Fixed with Col⁰· Carrington (the supervisor of the district) the surveys of Inspection for the District of this State
& named the characters for them—an acct. of which was
transmitted to the Secretary of the Treasury.

Dined at a public entertainment given by the Corporation of Richmond.

The buildings in this place have encreased a good deal
since I was here last, but they are not of the best kind,—
the number of Souls in the City are ———.

THURSDAY, 14th.

Left Richmond after an early breakfast — & passing
through Manchester received a Salute from cannon & an
Escort of Horse under the command of Captn. David
Meade Randolph as far as Osbornes[103] when I was met by

---

[103] A point between Richmond and Petersburgh, where troops under
the traitor Arnold, and the republicans, had a severe skirmish in April,
1781. A prisoner captured by Arnold at that time, was asked by him,

the Petersburgh horse & escorted to that place & partook of a Public dinner given by the Mayor & Corporation
and went to an Assembly in the evening for the occasion
at which there were between 60 & 70 ladies.

Petersburgh which is said to contain near 3000 Souls is
well situated for trade at present, but when the James River navigation is completed and the cut from Elizabeth River
to Pasquotauck effected it must decline & that very considerably.—At present it receives at the Inspections nearly
a third of the Tobacco exported from the whole State besides a considerable quantity of Wheat and flour—much of
the former being Manufactured at the Mills near the Town
—Chief of the buildings, in this town are under the hill &
unpleasantly situated, but the heights around it are agreeable.

The Road from Richmond to this place passes through a
poor country principally covered with Pine except the interval lands on the River which we left on our left.

FRIDAY, 15th.

Having suffered very much by the dust yesterday—and
finding that parties of Horse, & a number of other Gentlemen were intending to attend me part of the way to day,
I caused their enquiries respecting the time of my setting
out, to be answered that, I should endeavor to do it before

"If the Americans should catch me, what would they do with me?"
The soldier promptly replied, " They would bury with military honors
the leg which was wounded at Quebec and Saratoga, and hang the remainder of you upon a gibbet."

eight o'clock; but I did it a little after five, by which means I avoided the inconveniences above mentioned.

I came twelve miles to breakfast, at one Jesse Lee's, a tavern newly set up upon a small scale, and 15 miles farther to dinner; and where I lodged, at the House of one Oliver, which is a good one for horses, and where there are tolerable clean beds.—For want of proper stages I could go no farther.—The Road along whch. I travelled to day is through a level piney Country, until I came to Nottaway, [84] on which there seems to be some good land, the rest is very poor & seems scarce of Water.

Finding that the two horses wch. drew my baggage waggon were rather too light for the draught; and, (one of them especially) losing his flesh fast, I engaged two horses to be at this place this evening to carry it to the next stage 20 miles off in the morning, and sent them on led to be there ready for me.

SATURDAY, 16th.

Got into my Carriage a little after 5 o'clock, and travelled thro' a cloud of dust until I came within two or three miles of Hix's ford when it began to Rain.—Breakfasted at one Andrews' a small but decent House about a mile after passing the ford (or rather the bridge) over Meherrin River.—Although raining moderately, but with appearances of breaking up, I continued my journey—induced to it by the crouds which were coming into a general Muster at the Court House of Greensville, who would I presumed

---

[104] The Nottaway river. This with the Meherrin, forms the Chowan River, that empties into Albemarle Sound.

soon have made the Ho. I was in too noizy to be agreeable.
—I had not however rode two miles before it began to be
stormy, & to rain violently which, with some intervals, it
contind. to do the whole afternoon.—The uncomfortable-
ness of it, for Men & Horses, would have induced me to put
up ; but the only Inn short of Hallifax having no stables in
wch. the horses could be comfortable, & no Rooms or beds
which appeared tolerable, & every thing else having a dirty
appearance, I was compelled to keep on to Hallifax ; 27
miles from Andrews—48 from Olivers—and 75 from Petersburgh—At this place (i. e. Hallifax) I arrived about six
o'clock, after crossing the Roanoke ; on the South bank of
which it stands.

This River is crossed in flat Boats which take in a Carriage & four horses at once.—At this time, being low, the
water was not rapid but at times it must be much so, as it
frequently overflows its banks which appear to be at least
25 ft. perpendicular height.

The lands upon the River appear rich, & the low grounds
of considerable width—but those which lay between the
different Rivers—namely Appamattox, Nottaway, Meherrin
and Roanoke are all alike flat, poor & covered principaly
with pine timber.

It has already been observed that before the Rain fell, I
was travelling in a continued cloud of dust—but after it
had rained some time, the Scene was reversed, and my passage was through water ; so level are the Roads.

From Petersburg to Hallifax (in sight of the Road) are
but few good Houses, with small appearances of wealth.—
The lands are cultivated in Tobacco—Corn,—Wheat &

Oats, but Tobacco & the raising of Porke for market, seems to be the principal dependence of the Inhabitants; especially towards the Roanoke.—Cotton & Flax are also raised but not extensively.

Hallifax is the first town I came to after passing the line between the two States, and is about 20 miles from it.— To this place vessels by the aid of Oars & Setting poles are brought for the produce which comes to this place, and others along the River; and may be carried 8 or 10 miles higher to the falls which are neither great nor of much extent;—above these (which are called the great falls) there are others; but none but what may with a little improvement be passed. This town stands upon high ground; and it is the reason given for not placing it at the head of the navigation there being none but low ground between it and the falls—It seems to be in a decline & does not it is said contain a thousand Souls.

Sunday, 17th.

Col[o.] Ashe[105] the Representative of the district in which this town stands, and several other Gentlemen called upon, and invited me to partake of a dinner which the Inhabitants were desirous of seeing me at & excepting it dined with them accordingly.

---

[105] John B. Ashe, a soldier of the Revolution under Gen. Greene, a member of the Continental Congress in 1787, a representative of the Federal Congress from 1790 to 1793, and afterwards elected governor of the State. He died before entering upon the duties of the office.

MONDAY, 18th.

Set out by six o'clock—dined at a small house kept by one Slaughter, 22 Miles from Hallifax and lodged at Tarborough 14 Miles further.

This place is less than Hallifax, but more lively and thriving;—it is situated on Tar River which goes into Pamplico Sound and is crossed at the Town by means of a bridge a great height from the water, and notwithstanding the freshes rise sometimes nearly to the arch.—Corn, Porke, and some Tar are the exports from it.—We were recd. at this place by as good a salute as could be given by one piece of artillery.

TUESDAY, 19th.

At 6 o'clock I left Tarborough accompanied by some of the most respectable people of the place for a few miles—dined at a trifling place called Greenville 25 miles distant—and lodged at one Allan's 14 miles further a very indifferent house without stabling which for the first time since I commenced my Journey were obliged to stand without a cover.

Greenville is on Tar River and the exports the same as from Tarborough with a greater proportion of Tar—for the lower down the greater number of Tar makers are there — This article is contrary to all ideas one would entertain on the subject, rolled as Tobacco by an axis which goes through both heads—one horse draws two barrels in this manner.

WEDNESDAY, 20th.

Left Allans before breakfast, & under a misapprehension went to a Col⁰· Allans, supposing it to be public house; where we were very kindly & well entertained without knowing it was at his expence, until it was too late to rectify the mistake.—After breakfasting, & feeding our horses here, we proceeded on & crossing the River Neuse 11 miles further, arrived in Newbern to dinner.

At this ferry which is 10 miles from Newbern, we were met by a small party of Horse; the district Judge (Mr. Sitgreave) [106] and many of the principal Inhabitants of Newbern, who conducted us into town to exceeding good lodgings—It ought to have been mentioned that another small party of horse under one Simpson met us at Greensville, and in spite of every endeavor which could comport with decent civility, to excuse myself from it, they would attend me to Newbern.—Col⁰· Allan did the same.

This town is situated at the confluence of the Rivers Neuse & Trent, and though low is pleasant. Vessels drawing more than 9 feet water cannot get up loaded.—It stands on a good deal of ground, but the buildings are sparce and altogether of Wood;—some of which are large & look well—The number of Souls are about 2000.—Its exports consist of Corn, Tobacco, Pork,—but principally of Naval Stores & lumber.

---

[106] John Sitgreaves was a resident of Newbern, and had been an officer in the war for Independence. He was a member of the Continental Congress in 1784, of his State Legislature in 1787, and was made United States District Judge.

Thursday, 21st.

Dined with the Citizens at a public dinner given by them ; and went to a dancing assembly in the evening— both of which was at what they call the Pallace—formerly the Government House & a good brick building but now hastening to Ruins.[107]—The Company at both was numerous at the latter there were abt. 70 ladies.

This town by Water is about 70 miles from the Sea— but in a direct line to the entrance of the River not over 35—and to the nearest Seaboard not more than 20, or 25. —Upon the River Neuse, & 80 miles above Newbern, the Convention of the State that adopted the federal Constitution made choice of a spot, or rather district within which to fix their Seat of Government ; but it being lower than the back Members (of the Assembly) who hitherto have been most numerous inclined to have it they have found means to obstruct the measure—but since the Cession of

---

[107] This building was erected for Governor Tryon in 1769 ; and his demand upon the Assembly for twenty-five thousand dollars for the purpose of building a palace "suitable for the residence of the royal governor," was one of the causes of strong popular indignation against the governor. His wife and sister, both beautiful and accomplished women, used every blandishment to induce compliance on the part of the representatives of the people. Mrs. Tryon gave them princely dinners and balls. Human nature then, as now, was weak, and Tryon not only secured the first appropriation of $25,000, but a further sum of $50,000.

A drawing of the building, with a full account of it, may be found in Lossing's *Pictorial Field Book of the Revolution*, ii., 364, second edition.

their Western territory it is supposed that the matter will be revived to good effect.

FRIDAY, 22d.

Under an Escort of horse, and many of the principal Gentlemen of Newbern I recommenced my journey—dined at a place called Trenton which is the head of the boat navigation of the River Trent, wch. is crossed at this place on a bridge—and lodged at one Shrine's 10 m. farther—both indifferent Houses.

SATURDAY, 23d.

Breakfasted at one Everets 12 miles bated at a Mr. Foy's 12 miles farther and lodged at one Sage's 20 miles beyd. it—all indifferent Houses.

SUNDAY, 24th.

Breakfasted at an indifferent House about 13 miles from Sage's—and three miles further met a party of Light Horse from Wilmington; and after these a Commee. & other Gentlemen of the Town; who came out to escort me into it, and at which I arrived under a federal salute at very good lodgings prepared for me, about two o'clock—at these I dined with the Commee. whose company I asked.

The whole Road from Newbern to Wilmington (except in a few places of small extent) passes through the most barren country I ever beheld; especially in the parts nearest the latter; which is no other than a bed of white sand. —In places, however, before we came to these, if the ideas of poverty could be separated from the Sand, the appearances of it are agreeable, resembling a lawn well covered with evergreens, and a good verdure below from a broom or course grass which having sprung since the burning of the Woods had a neat and handsome look especially as there were parts entirely open—and others with ponds of water, which contributed not a little to the beauty of the scene.

Wilmington is situated on the Cape Fear River, about 30 miles *by water* from its mouth, but much less by land— It has some good houses pretty compactly built.—The whole undr. a hill ; which is formed entirely of sand.—The number of Souls in it amount by the enumeration to about 1000, but it is agreed on all hands that the Census in this State has been very inaccurately, & Shamefully taken by the Marshall's deputies ; who, instead of going to Peoples houses, & there, on the spot, ascertaining the Nos. ; have advertised a meeting of them at certain places, by which means those who did not attend (and it seems many purposely avoided doing it, some from an apprehension of its being introductory of a tax, & others from religious scruples) have gone with their families, unnumbered—In other instances, it is said these deputies have taken their information from the Captains of Militia Companies ; not only as to the men on their Muster Rolls, but of the Souls, in their respective families ; which at best, must in a variety of cases, be mere conjecture whilst all those who are not on their lists—Widows and their families &c. pass unnoticed.

Wilmington, unfortunately for it, has a Mud bank, —— miles below, over which not more than 10 feet water can be brought at common tides, yet it is said vessels of 250

Tons have come up.—The quty. of Shipping, which load here annually, amounts to about 1200 Tonns.—The exports consist chiefly of Naval Stores and lumber.—Some Tobacco, Corn, Rice, & flax seed with Porke.—It is at the head of the tide navigation, but inland navigation may be extended 115 miles farther to and above Fayettesville which is from Wilmington 90 miles by land, & 115 by Water as above.—Fayettesville is a thriving place containing near —— Souls—6000 Hhds. of Tobacco, & 3000 Hhds. of Flax Seed have been recd. at it in the course of the year.

Monday, 25th.

Dined with the Citizens of the place at a public dinner given by them—Went to a Ball in the evening at which there were 62 ladies—illuminations, Bonfires, &c.

Tuesday, 26th.

Having sent my Carriage across the day before, I left Wilmington about 6 o'clock, accompanied by most of the Gentlemen of the Town, and breakfasting at Mr. Ben. Smith's lodged at one Russ' 25 miles from Wilmington.— An indifferent House.

Wednesday, 27th.

Breakfasted at Willm. Gause's a little out of the direct Road 14 miles—crossed the boundary line between No. & South Carolina abt. half after 12 o'clock which is 10 miles from Gause's—dined at a private house (one Cochran's,) about 2 miles farther—and lodged at Mr. Vareen's 14

miles more and 2 miles short of the long bay.—To this
house we were directed as a Tavern, but the proprietor of
it either did not keep one, or would not acknowledge it—
we therefore were entertained (& very kindly) without
being able to make compensation.

THURSDAY, 28th.

Mr. Vareen piloted us across the Swash (which at high
water is impassable, & at times, by the shifting of the
Sands is dangerous) on the long Beach of the Ocean ; and
it being at a proper time of the tide we passed along it
with ease and celerity to the place of quitting it, which is
estimated 16 miles,—five miles farther we got dinner & fed
our horses at a Mr. Pauley's a private house, no public one
being on the Road ;—and being met on the Road, & kindly
invited by a Doctor Flagg to his house, we lodged there ;
it being about 10 miles from Pauley's & 33 from Vareen's.

FRIDAY, 29th.

We left Doctr. Flagg's about 6 o'clock, and arrived at
Captn. Wm. Alston's on the Waggamau[108] to Breakfast.

Captn. Alston is a Gentleman of large fortune and
esteemed one of the neatest Rice planters in the State of
So. Carolina and a proprietor of the most valuable ground
for the culture of this article.—His house which is large,
new, and elegantly furnished stands on a sand hill, high for
the Country, with his Rice fields below ; the contrast of

---

[108] Waccamaw.

which with the lands back of it, and the Sand & piney barrens through which we had passed is scarcely to be conceived.

At Captn. Alston's we were met by General Moultree, Col[o.] Washington[109] & Mr. Rutledge (son of the present Chief Justice of So. Carolina) who had come out that far to escort me to town.—We dined and lodged at this Gentlemans and Boats being provided we the next morning

SATURDAY, 30th.

Crossed the Waggamau to Georgetown by descending the River three miles—at this place we were recd. under a Salute of Cannon, & by a Company of Infantry handsomely uniformed.—I dined with the Citizens in public; and in the afternoon, was introduced to upwards of 50 ladies who had assembled (at a Tea party) on the occasion.

George Town seems to be in the shade of Charleston— It suffered during the War by the British, having had many of its Houses burnt.—It is situated on a pininsula betwn. the River Waccamaw & Sampton *Creek* about 15

---

[109] Colonel William Washington, the eminent cavalry officer in the southern campaign. He had invited the President, several months before he commenced his journey, to accept the hospitalities of his house in Charleston. "I cannot," replied the president, "without involving myself in inconsistency; as I have determined to pursue the same plan in my Southern—as I did in my Eastern visit, which was not to incommode any private family by taking up my quarters with them during my journey. It leaves me unencumbered by engagements, and by a uniform adherence to it, I shall avoid giving umbrage to any, by declining all such invitations."

miles from the Sea—a bar is to be passed, over which not more than 12 feet water can be brot. except at Spring tides; which (tho' the Inhabitants are willing to entertain different ideas,) must ever be a̋ considerable let to its importance; especially if the cut between the Santee & Cooper Rivers, should ever be accomplished.

The Inhabitants of this place (either unwilling or unable) could give no account of the number of Souls in it, but I should not compute them at more than 5 or 600.—Its chief export, Rice.

SUNDAY, MAY FIRST.

Left Georgetown about 6 o'clock and crossing the Santee Creek at the Town, and the Santee River 12 miles from it, at Lynch's Island, we breakfasted and dined at Mrs. Horry's about 15 miles from Georgetown & lodged at the Plantation of Mr. Manigold[110] about 19 miles farther.

MONDAY, 2d.

Breakfasted at the Country seat of Govr. Pinckney[111] about

---

[110] Manigault. It is related of one of this family (who were descendants of French Protestant refugees who settled in South Carolina), that while the siege of Charleston by the British, in 1780, was progressing, a lighted bomb fell near him, within the breastwork. He caught it up instantly, and throwing it into a wet ditch outside, exclaimed, "What for you smoke your pipe here?"

[111] Charles Pinckney, one of the delegates in the convention that framed the Federal Constitution. He was governor of his State at three different periods; a Senator of the United States, and minister to Spain.

18 miles from our lodging place, & then came to the ferry
at Haddrel's point, 6 miles further, where I was met by the
Recorder of the City, Genl. Pinckney & Edward Rutledge,
Esqr. in a 12 oared barge rowed by 12 American Captains
of Ships, most elegantly dressed.—There were a great
number of other Boats with Gentlemen and ladies in them;
—and two Boats with Music; all of whom attended me
across, and on the passage were met by a number of others.
—As we approached the town a salute with artillery commenced, and at the Wharf I was met by the Governor, the
Lt. Governor, the Intendt. of the City;—the two Senators
of the State, Wardens of the City—Cincinnati, &c. &c. and
conducted to the Exchange where they passed by in
procession—from thence I was conducted in like manner to
my lodgings—after which I dined at the Governors (in
what he called a private way) with 15 or 18 Gentlemen.

It may as well in this as in any other place, be observed,
that the Country from Wilmington through which the
Road passes, is, except in very small spots, much the same
as what has already been described; that is to say, sand
& pine barrens—with very few inhabitants—we were
indeed informed that at some distance from the Road on
both sides the land was of a better quality, & thicker
settled, but this could only be on the Rivers & larger
waters—for a perfect sameness seems to run through all
the rest of the Country—on these—especially the swamps
and low lands on the Rivers, the Soil is very rich; and
productive when reclaimed; but to do this is both labori-
ous and expensive.—The Rice planters have two modes of
watering their fields—the first by the tide—the other by

resurvoirs drawn from the adjacent lands.—The former is
best because most certain.—A crop without either is
precarious,—because a drought may not only injure, but
destroy it.—Two and an half and 3 barrels to the Acre is
esteemed a good Crop and 8 or 10 Barrls. for each grown
hand is very profitable; but some have 12 & 14, whilst
5 or 6 is reckoned the average production of a hand—a
barrel contains about 600 weight and the present price is
about ¹⁰/₆ & ¹¹/ Sterg. pr. 100.

The lodgings provided for me in this place were very
good, being the furnished house of a Gentleman at present
in the Country; but occupied by a person placed there on
purpose to accomodate me, & who was paid in the same
manner as any other letter of lodgings would have been
paid.

Tuesday, 3d.

Breakfasted with Mrs. Rutledge (the Lady of the Chief
Justice of the State who was on the Circuits) and dined
with the Citizens at a public dinr. given by them at the
Exchange.

Was visited about 2 o'clock, by a great number of the
most respectable ladies of Charleston—the first honor of
the kind I had ever experienced and it was as flattering as
it was singular.

Wednesday, 4th.

Dined with the Members of the Cincinnati, and in the
evening went to a very elegant dancing Assembly at the
Exchange—At which were 256 elegantly dressed & handsome ladies.

In the forenoon (indeed before breakfast to day) I visited and examined the lines of attack & defence of the City and was satisfied that the defence was noble & honorable altho' the measure was undertaken upon wrong principles and impolitic.[112]

Thursday, 5th.

Visited the works of Fort Johnson James' Island, and Fort Moultree on Sullivans Island;—both of which are in Ruins, and scarcely a trace of the latter left—the former quite fallen.

Dined with a very large Company at the Governor's & in the evening went to a Concert at the Exchange at wch. there were at least 400 ladies the number & appearance of wch. exceeded any thing of the kind I had ever seen.

Friday, 6th.

Viewed the town on horseback by riding through most of the principal Streets.

Dined at Majr. Butler's and went to a Ball in the evening at the Governors where there was a select Company of ladies.

Saturday, 7th.

Before break (fast) I visited the Orphan House at which there were one hundred & seven boys & girls —This appears to be a charitable institution and under good

---

[112] These lines were upon Charleston Neck, extending from the Ashley to the Cooper river, at the junction of which the city stands.

management.—I also viewed the City from the balcony of ——— Church from whence the whole is seen in one view and to advantage, the Gardens & green trees which are interspersed adding much to the beauty of the prospect. Charleston stands on a Pininsula between the Ashley & Cooper Rivers and contains about 1600 dwelling houses and nearly 16.000 Souls of which about 8000 are white—It lies low with unpaved streets (except the footways) of sand. —There are a number of very good houses of Brick & wood but most of the latter—The Inhabitants are wealthy, —Gay—& hospitable; appear happy and satisfied with the Genl. Government. A cut is much talked off between the Ashley & Santee Rivers but it would seem I think, as if the accomplishment of the measure was not very near—It would be a great thing for Charleston if it could be effected.—The principal exports from this place is Rice, Indigo, and Tobacco; of the last from 5 to 8000 Hhds. have been exported, and of the first from 80 to 120,000 Barrels.

SUNDAY, 8th.

Went to Crowded Churches in the morning & afternoon. to ——— in the morning & ——— in the afternoon. Dined with General Moultree.

MONDAY, 9th.

At six o'clock I recommenced my journey for Savanna; attended by a Corps of the Cincinnati and most of the principal Gentlemen of the City as far as the bridge over Ashley River, where we breakfasted, and proceeded to

Col⁰· W. Washington's at Sandy-hill with a select party of particular friends—distant from Charleston 28 miles.

Tuesday, 10th.

Took leave of all my friends and attendants at this place (except General Moultree & Majr. Butler the last of whom intended to accompany me to Savanna, and the other to Purisburgh,[113] at which I was to be met by Boats,) & breakfasting at Judge Bee's 12 miles from Sandy Hill, lodged at Mr. Obrian Smith's 18 or 20 further on.

Wednesday, 11th.

After an early breakfast at Mr. Smiths we road 20 miles to a place called Pokitellieo[114] where a dinner was provided by the Parishoners of Prince William for my reception, and an address from them was presented and answered.— After dinner we proceeded 16 miles farther to Judge Hayward's where we lodged, &, as also at Mr. Smith's were kindly and hospitably ▸entertained.—My going to Col⁰· Washington's is to be ascribed to motives of friendship & relationship ; but to Mr. Smith's & Judge Haywards to those of necessity ; their being no public houses on the Road and my distance to get to these private ones increased at least 10 or 12 miles between Charleston and Savanna.

---

[113] Purysburg, on the Savannah river, named in honor of John Pury, founder of a Swiss settlement in South Carolina. It was Lincoln's head-quarters for a while, early in 1779.

[114] Pocotaligo, on the Combahee river, Beaufort District, South Carolina.

THURSDAY, 12th.

By five o'clock we set out from Judge Hayward's, and road to Purisburgh 22 miles to breakfast.

At that place I was met by Messrs. Jones, Col°· Habersham, Mr. Jno. Houston, Genl. Mc.Intosh and Mr. Clay,[115] a Comee. from the City of Savanna to conduct me thither. —Boats also were ordered there by them for my accomodation; among which a handsome 8 oared barge rowed by 8 American Captns. attended.—In my way down the River I called upon Mrs. Green the Widow of the deceased Genl. Green, (at a place called Mulberry Grove) & asked her how she did.[116]—At this place (2 miles from Purisburgh) my horses and Carriages were landed, and had 12 miles farther by Land to Savanna.—The wind & tide being both agst. us, it was 6 o'clock before we reached the City where we were received under every demonstration that could be given of joy & respect.—We were Seven

---

[115] Noble Wimberly Jones, Joseph Habersham, John Houston, Lachlin McIntosh, and Joseph Clay, all eminent patriots during the Revolution.

[116] The State of Georgia gave General Nathaniel Greene quite a large tract of land in testimony of appreciation for his services in the Southern campaigns of the Revolution. He went to Georgia in 1785, to look after his estate; while walking one day, in June, 1786, without an umbrella, he was "sun struck," and died on the 19th of that month, at the age of forty-six years. His widow occupied the property until her death. There, under the roof of that hospitable lady, in 1792 or '93, Eli Whitney, the inventor of the cotton-gin, planned and constructed his first machine; and at that home, in 1807, the daughter of General Greene, received the brass cannon, captured at Eutaw Springs, which Congress voted to her gallant father.

hours making the passage which is often performed in 4, tho' the computed distance is 25 miles—Illumns. at night.

I was conducted by the Mayor & Wardens to very good lodging which had been provided for the occasion, and partook of a public dinner given by the Citizens at the Coffee Room.—At Purisburgh I parted with Genl. Moultree.

FRIDAY, 13th.

Dined with the Members of the Cincinnati at a public dinner given at the same place—and in the evening went to a dancing Assembly at which there was about 100 well dressed & handsome ladies.

SATURDAY, 14th.

A little after 6 o'clock, in Company with Genl. McIntosh, Genl. Wayne, the Mayor and many others (principal Gentlemen of the City,) I visited the City, and the attack & defence of it in the year 1779, under the combined forces of France and the United States, commanded by the Count de Estaing & Genl. Lincoln.[117]—To form an opinion of the attack at this distance of time, and the change which has taken place in the appearance of the ground by the cutting away of the woods, &c. is hardly to be done with justice to the subject; especially as there is remaining scarcely any of the defences.

Dined to day with a number of the Citizens (not less

---

[117] Traces of these lines of defence are still visible in the rear of the town. For an account of their appearance as late as 1848, see Lossing's *Pictorial Field Book of the Revolution*, ii., 531, second edition.

than 200) in an elegant Bower erected for the occasion on
the Bank of the River below the Town.—In the evening
there was a tolerable good display of fireworks.

SUNDAY, 15th.

After morning Service, and receiving a number of visits
from the most respectable ladies of the place (as was the
case yesterday) I set out for Augusta, Escorted beyd. the
limits of the City by most of the Gentlemen in it, and din-
ing at Mulberry Grove the Seat of Mrs. Green,—lodged at
one Spencers—distant 15 miles.

Savanna stands upon what may be called high ground
for this Country—It is extremely Sandy wch. makes the
walking very disagreeable; & the houses uncomfortable in
warm & windy weather, as they are filled with dust whenever these happen.—The town on 3 sides is surrounded
with cultivated Rice fields which have a rich and luxuriant
appearance. On the 4th or backside it is a fine sand.—
The harbour is said to be very good, & often filled with
square rigged vessels, but there is a bar below over which
not more than 12 water can be brot. except at sprg. tides.
—The tide does not flow above 12 or 14 miles above the
City though the River is swelled by it more than double
that distance.—Rice & Tobacco (the last of wch. is greatly
increasing) are the principal Exports—Lumber & Indigo
are also Exported, but the latter is on the decline, and it is
supposed by Hemp & Cotton.—Ship timber. viz: live Oak
& Cedar, is (and may be more so) valuable in the exptn.

Monday, 16th.

Breakfasted at Russells—15 miles from Spencer's—dined at Garnets 19 further & lodged at Pierces 8 miles more, in all—42 miles to day.

Tuesday, 17th.

Breakfasted at Spinner's 17 miles—dined at Lamberts 13—and lodged at Waynesborough (wch. was coming 6 miles out of our way) 14, in all 43 miles—Waynésborough is a small place, but the Seat of the Court of Burkes County—6 or 8 dwelling houses is all it contains;—an attempt is making (without much apparent effect) to establish an Academy at it as is the case also in all the Counties.

Wednesday, 18th.

Breakfasted at Tulcher's 15 miles from Waynesborough; and within 4 miles of Augusta met the Govor. (Telfair), Judge Walton,[118] the Attorney Genl. & most of the principal Gentlemen of the place; by whom I was escorted into the Town, & recd. under a discharge of Artillery,—the distance I came to day was about 32 miles—Dined with a large Company at the Governors, & drank Tea there with many well dressed Ladies.

The Road from Savanna to Augusta is, for the most

---

[118] George Walton, one of the signers of the Declaration of Independence. A fine monument stands in Augusta, erected to the memory of Walton and his Georgia colleagues who signed that instrument.

part, through Pine barrens; but more uneven than I had been accustomed to since leavg. Petersburgh in Virginia, especially after riding about 30 miles from the City of that name; here & there indeed, a piece of Oak land is passed on this Road, but of small extent & by no means of the first quality.

Thursday, 19th.

Received & answered an Address from the Citizens of Augusta;—dined with a large Company of them at their Court Ho.—and went to an Assembly in the evening at the Accadamy; at which there were between 60 & 70 well dressed ladies.

Friday, 20th.

Viewed the Ruins, or rather small Remns. of the Works which had been erected by the British during the War and taken by the Americans.—Also the falls, which are about 2 miles above the Town;—and the Town itself.

These falls (as they are called) are nothing more than rapids.—They are passable in their present state by boats with skilful hands, but may at a very small expence be improved, by removing a few rocks only, to streighten the passage.—Above them there is good boat navigation for many miles; by which the produce may be, & in some measure is, transported.—At this place, i. e. the falls, the good lands begin; & encrease in quality to the westward & No.ward.—All below them, except the Interval lands on the Rivers and Rice Swamps which extend from them, the whole Country is a Pine barren.—The town of Augusta is well laid out with wide & spacious Streets.—It stands on a large area of a perfect plain but it is not yet thickly built tho' surprizingly so for the time; for in 1783 there were not more than half a dozen dwelling houses; now there are not less than ——— containing about ——— Souls of which about ——— are blacks.—It bids fair to be a large Town being at the head of the *present* navigation, & a fine Country back of it for support, which is settling very fast by Tobacco planters.—The culture of which article is encreaseing very fast, and bids fair to be the principal export from the State; from this part of it, it certainly will be so.

Augusta, though it covers more ground than Savanna, does not contain as many Inhabitants the latter having by the late census between 14 & 1500 hundred whites and about 800 blacks.

Dined at a private dinner with Govr. Telfair to day; and gave him dispatches for the Spanish Govr. of East Florida, respecting the Countenance given by that Governt. to the fugitive Slaves of the Union—wch. dispatches were to be forwarded to Mr. Seagrove, Collector of St. Mary's, who was requested to be the bearer of them, and instructed to make arrangements for the prevention of these evils and, if possible, for the restoration of the property— especially of those slaves wch. had gone off since the orders of the Spanish Court, to discountenance this practice of recg. them.

SATURDAY, 21st.

Left Augusta about 6 o'clock, and takg. leave of the Governor & principal Gentlemen of the place at the bridge over Savanna River, where they had assembled for the purpose, I proceeded in Company with Col[os.] Hampton[119] & Taylor, & Mr. Lithgow a committee from Columbia, (who had come on to meet & conduct me to that place) & a Mr. Jameson from the Village of Granby on my Rout.

Dined at a house about 20 miles from Augusta and lodged at one Odem, about 20 miles farther.

SUNDAY, 22d.

Rode about 21 miles to breakfast, and passing through the village of Granby[120] just below the first falls in the Congaree (which was passed in a flat bottomed boat at a Rope ferry,) I lodged at Columbia, the newly adopted Seat of the Government of South Carolina about 3 miles from it, on the No. side of the River, and 27 from my breakfasting stage.

The whole Road from Augusta to Columbia is a pine barren of the worst sort, being hilly as well as poor.—This circumstance added to the distance, length of the stages,

---

[119] Colonel Wade Hampton, a meritorious officer in the Southern Army of the Revolution, and a commander on the northern frontier of New York in the War of 1812.

[120] The site of Fort Granby, a dwelling fortified by the British, as a link in a chain of military posts from Camden to Charleston. It was captured by Colonel Lee, of the famous partisan "Legion," in May, 1781.

want of water and heat of the day, foundered one of my horses very badly.

Beyond Granby 4 miles I was met by sevl. Gentlemen of that place & Wynnsborough ; and on the banks of the River on the No. side by a number of others, who escorted me to Columbia.

MONDAY, 23d.

Dined at a public dinner in the State house with a number of Gentlemen & Ladies of the Town of Columbia, & Country round about to the amt. of more than 150, of which 50 or 60 were of the latter.

TUESDAY, 24th.

The condition of my foundered horse obliged me to remain at this place, contrary to my intention, this day also.

Columbia is laid out upon a large scale ; but, in my opinion, had better been placed on the River below the falls.—It is now an uncleared wood, with very few houses in it, and those all wooden ones—The State House (which is also of wood) is a large and commodious building, but unfinished—The Town is on dry, but cannot be called high ground, and though surrounded by Piney & Sandy land is, itself, good—The State house is near two miles from the River, at the confluence of the Broad River & Saluda.— From Granby the River is navigable for Craft which will, when the River is a little swelled, carry 3000 bushels of Grain—when at its usual heighth less, and always some.— The River from hence to the Wateree below which it takes the name of the Santee is very crooked ;[121] it being, according to the computed distance near 400 miles—Columbia from Charleston is 130 miles.

WEDNESDAY, 25th.

Set out at 4 o'clock for Camden—(the foundered horse being led slowly on)—breakfasted at an indifferent house 22 miles from the town, (the first we came to) and reached Camden about two o'clock, 14 miles further, when an address was recd. & answered.—Dined (late with a number of Gentlemen & Ladies at a public dinner.—The Road from Columbia to Camden, excepting a mile or two at each place, goes over the most miserable pine barren I ever saw, being quite a white sand, & very hilly.—On the Wateree within a mile & half of which the town stands the lands are very good,—they Culture Corn, Tobacco & Indigo.—Vessels carrying 50 or 60 Hhds. of Tobo. come up to the Ferry at this place at which there is a Tobacco Wharehouse.

THURSDAY, 26th.

After viewing the british works about Camden I set out for Charlotte—on my way—two miles from Town—I examined the ground on wch. Genl. Green & Lord Rawdon had their action.[122]—The ground had but just been taken

---

121 At Buck's Head Neck, near Fort Motte, just above the junction of the Congaree and Wateree (which form the Santee), the Congaree makes a sweep of eight miles and approaches itself to within the distance of a quarter of a mile.

122 On Hobkirk's Hill, April 25, 1781.

by the former—was well chosen—but he not well established in it before he was attacked ; which by capturing a Videt was, in some measure by surprise—Six miles further on I came to the ground where Genl. Gates & Lord Cornwallis had their Engagement wch. terminated so unfavourably for the former.[123]—As this was a night meeting of both Armies on their march, & altogether unexpected each formed on the ground they met without any advantage in it on either side it being level & open.—Had Genl. Gates been ½ a mile further advanced, an impenetrable Swamp would have prevented the attack which was made on him by the British Army, and afforded him time to have formed his own plans ; but having no information of Lord Cornwallis's designs, and perhaps not being apprised of this advantage it was not seized by him.

Camden is a small place with appearances of some new buildings.—It was much injured by the British whilst in their possession.[121]

After halting at one Sutton's 14 m. from Camden I lodged at James Ingrams 12 miles father.

---

[123] On the north side of Sanders's Creek, August 16, 1780. The two generals were approaching each other in the night, along a road filled with deep sand ; and neither of them had any knowledge of the fact, until their advanced guards came in contact. The battle occurred early in the morning.

[124] Lord Rawdon, the British commander there, alarmed for the safety of his forts in the lower country, set fire to Camden on the 10th of May, 1781, and retreated down the Santee.

FRIDAY, 27th.

Left Ingrams about 4 o'clock, and breakfasting at one Barr's 18 miles distant lodged at Majr. Crawford's 8 miles farther—About 2 miles from this place I came to the Corner where the No. Carolina line comes to the Rd.—from whence the Road is the boundary for 12 miles more.—At Majr. Crawfords I was met by some of the chiefs of the Catawba nation who seemed to be under apprehension that some attempts were making, or would be made to deprive them of part of the 40,000 Acres wch. was secured to them by Treaty and wch. is bounded by this Road.[125]

---

[125] This is yet a reservation for the Catawba Indians, near the southeast corner of Yorkville district, in South Carolina. It was originally larger than now. They were once a powerful tribe, but are dwindled to the most insignificant remnant. Their chief village was on the Catawba river, about twenty-five miles from Yorkville. The following eloquent petition of Peter Harris, a Catawba warrior during the Revolution, is preserved among the Colonial records at Columbia, South Carolina. It is dated, 1822:

"I am one of the lingering survivors of an almost extinguished race. Our graves will soon be our only habitations. I am one of the few stalks that still remain in the field where the tempest of the Revolution has passed. I fought against the British for your sake. The British have disappeared, and you are free; yet from me have the British took nothing; nor have I gained any thing by their defeat. I pursued the deer for subsistence; the deer are disappearing, and I must starve. God ordained me for the forest, and my ambition is the shade. But the strength of my arm decays, and my feet fail me in the chase. The hand which fought for your liberties is now open for your relief. In my youth I bled in battle, that you might be independent; let not my heart in my old age bleed for the want of your commiseration."

Saturday, 28th.

Sett off from Crawfords by 4 o'clock and breakfasting at one Harrison's 18 miles from it got into Charlotte 13 miles further, before 3 oclock,—dined with Genl. Polk and a small party invited by him, at a Table prepared for the purpose.[126]

It was not, until I had got near Barrs that I had quit the Piney & Sandy lands—nor until I had got to Crawfords before the lands took quite a different complexion— here they began to assume a very rich look.

Charlotte is a trifling place, though the Court of Mecklenburg is held in it—There is a School (called a College) in it at which, at times there has been 50 or 60 boys.[127]

Sunday, 29th.

Left Charlotte about 7 o'clock, dined at Col⁰· Smiths 15 miles off, and lodged at Majr. Fifers 7 miles farther.

---

126 General Thomas Polk, who was Colonel of the militia of Mecklenburg County, North Carolina, at the opening of the war for Independence. It was in Charlotte, and partially under the influence and through the exertions of General Polk, that a convention of delegates, selected by the people of Mecklenburg County, passed resolutions at the close of May, 1775, which virtually declared the people represented free and independent of the British crown.

127 This was called, previous to the Revolution, Queen's Museum or College. There the republicans of that section of North Carolina met to discuss the exciting questions of the day. It was the Faneuil Hall of Western Carolina.

MONDAY, 30th.

At 4 o'clock I was out from Majr. Fifers ;[128] and in about 10 miles at the line which divides Mecklenburgh from Rowan Counties ; I met a party of horse belonging to the latter, who came from Salisbury to escort me on—(It ought to have been mentioned also that upon my entering the State of No. Carolina I was met by a Party of the Mecklenburgh horse—but these being near their homes I dismissed them)—I was also met 5 miles from Salisbury by the Mayor of, the Corporation, Judge Mc. Kòy, & many others ;—Mr. Steel, Representative for the district,[129] was so polite as to come all the way to Charlotte to meet me.— We arrived at Salisbury about 8 o'clock, to breakfast,—20 miles from Captn. Fifers.—The lands between Charlotte & Salisbury are very fine, of a reddish cast and well timbered, with but very little underwood—Between these two places

---

[128] Son of John Phifer, one of the leading patriots of Mecklenburg County, who died early in the Revolution. His remains were buried at the Red Hills, three miles west of Concord, in Cabarrus County, North Carolina. I saw over his grave in 1848, a rough, mutilated memorial slab, upon which, tradition averred, a fire was built by British soldiers, when on their march from Charlotte to Salisbury, in contempt for the patriot's memory. He was one of the signers of the Mecklenburg Declaration of Independence.

[129] General John Steele, who was a representative in Congress for four years. He was a native of Salisbury, and first appeared in public life as a member of the North Carolina House of Commons, in 1787. He was appointed by President Washington, controller of the United States Treasury, and was continued in office by President Adams. He died in 1815.

are the first meadows I have seen on the Road since I left Virga. & here also we appear to be getting into a Wheat Country.

This day I foundered another of my horses.

Dined at a public dinner givn. by the Citizens of Salisbury; & in the afternoon drank Tea at the same place with about 20 ladies, who had been assembled for the occasion.

Salisbury is but a small place altho' it is the County town, and the district Court is held in it;—nor does it appear to be much on the increase,—there is about three hundred souls in it and tradesmen of different kinds.

Tuesday, 31st.

Left Salisbury about 4 o'clock; at 5 miles crossed the Yadkin,[130] the principal stream of the Pedee, and breakfasted on the No. Bank, (while my Carriages & horses were crossing) at a Mr. Youngs' fed my horses 10 miles farther, at one Reeds—and about 3 o'clock (after another halt) arrived at Salem, one of the Moravian towns 20 miles farther—In all 35 from Salisbury.

The Road between Salisbury & Salem passes over very little good land, and much that is different; being a good deal mixed with Pine, but not sand.

Salem is a small but neat village; & like all the rest of

---

[130] At the Trading Ford, probably, where Greene with Morgan and his light troops crossed, with Cornwallis in pursuit. There is now a great bridge over the Yadkin, on the Salisbury road, about a mile and a half above the Trading Ford.

the Moravian settlements, is governed by an excellent
police—having within itself all kinds of artizans—The
number of Souls does not exceed 200.[131]

---

[131] There is still a very flourishing settlement of Moravians, or
United Brethren, at Salem, where the church was first planted in 1765.
The log-house in which the first Moravian settlers were at first lodged,
was yet standing in 1857.

Washington's visit as recorded in his Diary, is duly noted in the
records of the Moravian Society at Salem, and copies of the addresses
delivered on that occasion are preserved.

The following is the address of the Moravians to the President:—

" Happy in sharing the honor of a visit from the illustrious President
of the Union to the Southern States, the Brethren of Wachovia humbly
beg leave, upon this joyful occasion, to express their highest esteem,
duty, and affection, for the great patriot of this country.

" Deeply impressed as we are with gratitude to the great Author of
our being for his unbounded mercies, we cannot but particularly
acknowledge his gracious providence over the temporal and political
prosperity of the country, in the peace whereof we do find peace, and
wherein none can take a warmer interest than ourselves ; in particular,
when we consider that the same Lord who preserved your precious
person in so many imminent dangers has made you, in a conspicuous
manner, an instrument in his hands to forward that happy constitution,
together with those improvements, whereby our United States begin
to flourish, over which you preside with the applause of a thankful
nation.

" Whenever, therefore, we solicit the protection of the Father of
mercies over this favored country, we cannot but fervently implore his
kindness for your preservation, which is so intimately connected
therewith.

" May this gracious Lord vouchsafe to prolong your valuable life
as a further blessing, and an ornament of the constitution, that by your
worthy example the regard for religion be increased, and the improvements of civil society encouraged.

" The settlements of the United Brethren, though small, will always
make it their study to contribute as much as in them lie ; to the peace and

WEDNESDAY.

JUNE, 1st.

Having received information that Governor Martin was on his way to meet me; and would be at Salem this evening, I resolved to await his arrival at this place instead of halting a day at Guilford as I had intended;

Spent the forenoon in visiting the Shops of the different

---

improvement of the United States, and all the particular parts they live in, joining their ardent prayers to the best wishes of this whole continent, that your personal as well as domestic happiness may abound, and a series of successes may crown your labors for the prosperity of our times and an example to future ages, until the glorious reward of a faithful servant shall be your portion.

"Signed, in behalf of the United Brethren in Wachovia;

"FREDERICK WILLIAM MARSHALL,
"JOHN DANIEL KÖHLER,
"CHRISTIAN LEWIS BENZIEN.

"*Salem, the 1st of June,* 1791."

To which the President of the United States was pleased to return the following answer:—

" *To the United Brethren of Wachovia :*

"GENTLEMEN : I am greatly indebted to your respectful and affectionate expression of regard, and I am not less obliged by the patriotic sentiment contained in your address.

" From a society whose governing principles are industry and the love of order, much may be expected towards the improvement and prosperity of the country in which their settlements are formed, and experience authorizes the belief that much will be obtained.

" Thanking you with grateful sincerity for your prayers in my behalf, I desire to assure you of my best wishes for your social and individual happiness.

"G. WASHINGTON."

Tradesmen—The houses of accomodation for the single men & Sisters of the Fraternity—& their place of worship. —Invited six of their principal people to dine with me— and in the evening went to hear them sing, & perform on a variety of instruments Church music.

In the Afternoon Governor Martin as was expected (with his Secretary) arrived.[132]

---

[132] This entry closes this volume of the Diary. The President reached Mount Vernon on the 12th of June, having made a most satisfactory journey of more than seventeen hundred miles, from his seat on the Potomac, in sixty-six days, with the same team of horses. " My return to this place is sooner than I expected," he wrote to Hamilton, " owing to the uninterruptedness of my journey by sickness, from bad weather, or accidents of any kind whatsoever," for which he had made an allowance of eight days.

WASHINGTON'S

JOURNAL OF A TOUR TO THE OHIO,

IN 1753.

———————

With Notes by John G. Shea.

INTRODUCTION.

The earliest of Washington's diaries, printed almost as soon as its last page was written, possesses uncommon interest, from the fulness with which he describes the events of his journey,— a fulness for which we are indebted to the instructions of Governor Dinwiddie.

Washington was then twenty-one, but already a "person of distinction." Adjutant-general of the colonial troops, with the rank of major, to him was committed the northern division of the colony. His earlier exploration as surveyor had brought him into contact with the Indians, and none seemed better to know and understand them; while his early maturity, dignity, and judgment, fitted him for any important undertaking that did not require the experience of years.

Affairs had reached a crisis. France had colonized Canada, Illinois, and Louisiana, and connected them by detached posts, but the possession of the Ohio, so necessary to the safety of her wide provincial power, was soon to fall into the hands of her rival by the rapid progress of English colonization. To set a barrier to its westward progress, France determined to run a line of forts from Niagara to the forks of the Ohio, and down that river.

The Indians first took the alarm. When the tidings reached the Ohio that a French force was on its way to erect this line of forts, a council of the wandering tribes, Mingoes, Shawnees,

and Delawares, met at Logstown, and in April, 1753, dispatched an envoy to Niagara, to protest against the action of the
French. The protest was unheeded. Tanacharisson then went
to Fort Presque Isle to meet Marin, and reported to Washington,
as we shall see, the result of his fruitless mission.

Pennsylvania then took the alarm, and Governor Hamilton
in vain urged his assembly to check the French invasion of their
frontiers, yet they appointed Norris their speaker, and Franklin, to meet at Carlisle a deputation from the tribes. There
the Indian declared his will. The land was theirs. They
wished neither English nor French to intrude. Yet as danger
from the latter seemed more imminent, they were willing to
help the English to expel the French. They did not see that
it was but a change of masters, and if in the event English garrisons replaced the French, the power of the latter was scarcely prostrated, when, in 1763, the long-smothered wrath of the
baffled red man, swept the English from Forts Erie, Le Bœuf,
and Venango, and burst in its might on Fort Pitt.

Virginia, too, moved, and Washington, from his official position and his knowledge of the Indians, was selected by Governor Dinwiddie to proceed to the Ohio, demand the withdrawal of the French, and examine the condition of their forces.
The following letter, recently come to light, and one of the few
of that period of his career known, shows how he was engaged
when chosen for the mission to the Ohio.

WINCHESTER, Oct. 17, 1753.

HONORABLE SIR :—Last night, by return of the express who
went to Capt. Montour, I received the inclosed from Mr. Harris, at Susquehanna. I think no means should be neglected to
preserve what few Indians still remain in our interest, for which
reason I shall send Mr. Gist, as soon as he arrives, which I expect will be to-day, to Harris' Ferry, in hopes of engaging and

bringing with him the Belt of Wampum and other Indians at that place; and I shall further desire him to send an Indian express to Andrew Montour, to try if he can be brought along with him. In however trifling light the French attempting to alienate the affections of our Southern Indians may at first sight appear, I must look upon it as a thing of the utmost consequence, that requires our greatest and most immediate attention. I have often wondered at not hearing that this was attempted before, and had it noted, among other memoranda, to acquaint your honor of when I should come down. The French policy in treating with Indians is so prevalent, that I should not be in the least surprised were they to engage the Cherokees, Cuttabas, &c., unless timely and vigorous measures are taken to prevent it. A pusillanimous behavior would ill suit the times, and trusting for traders and common interpreters (who will sell their integrity to the highest bidder) may prove the destruction of these affairs. I therefore think, that if a person of distinction, acquainted with their language, is to be found, his price should be come to at any rate; if no such can be had, a man of sense and character to conduct the Indians to any council that may be had, or to superintend any other matters, will be extremely necessary.

It is impertinent, I own, in me to offer my opinions on these matters when better judges may direct; but my steady and hearty zeal in the cause, and the great impositions I have known practised by the traders, &c., upon these occasions, would not suffer me to be quite silent. I have heard, from undoubted authority, that some of the Cherokees that have been introduced as Sachems and Princes by the interpreters (who share their presents and profits), have been no others than common hunters and bloodthirsty villains. We have no accounts yet of the militia from Fairfax, &c. This day I march with about one hundred men to Fort Cumberland. Yesterday, by an express,

I was informed of the arrival of eighty odd recruits to Fredericksburgh, which I have ordered to proceed to this place, but for want of the regularity being observed, by which I should know where every officer, &c., ought to be, my orders are only conditional and always confused. Whatever necessarys your Honor gets below I should be glad to have them sent to Alexandria, from whence they come much more handy than from Fredericksburgh; besides, as provisions are lodged there, and none at the other place, it will be best for the men to be all sent there that is any ways convenient, for we have met with insuperable difficulty at Fredericksburgh, in our march from here, by the neglect of the Com., who is at this time greatly wanted here. Therefore, I hope your Honor will order him up immediately.

I am, Honorable Sir,

Your most obedient servant,

G. WASHINGTON.

But before this could have reached the governor, and been acted upon, came his commission, with these

Instructions for George Washington.

Whereas I have received information of a body of French forces being assembled in a hostile manner on the river Ohio, intending by force of arms, to erect certain forts on the said river, within this territory, and contrary to the dignity and peace of our sovereign, the King of Great Britain. These are therefore to require and direct you, the said George Washington, forthwith to repair to Logstown on the said river Ohio; and having there informed yourself where the said French forces have posted themselves, thereupon to proceed to such place; and being there arrived, to present your credentials, together with my letter to the chief commanding officer, and in the name of his Britannic Majesty, to demand an answer thereto.

On your arrival at Logstown you are to address yourself to the Half-King, to Monacatoocha, and other the Sachems of the Six Nations, acquainting them with your orders to visit and deliver my letter to the French commanding officer, and desiring the said chiefs to appoint you a sufficient number of their warriors to be your safeguard, as near the French as you may desire, and to wait your further direction.

You are diligently to inquire into the numbers and force of the French on the Ohio, and the adjacent country; how they are likely to be assisted from Canada; and what are the difficulties and conveniences of that communication, and the time required for it.

. You are to take care to be truly informed what forts the French have erected, and where; how they are garrisoned and appointed, and what is their distance from each other, and from Logstown; and from the best intelligence you can procure, you are to learn what gave occasion to this expedition of the French; how they are likely to be supported, and what their pretensions are.

When the French commandant has given you the required and necessary dispatches, you are to desire of him a proper guard to protect you as far on your return, as you may judge for your safety, against any straggling Indians or hunters, that may be ignorant of your character, and molest you.

Wishing you success in your negotiation, and a safe and speedy return, I am, &c.

ROBERT DINWIDDIE.

WILLIAMSBURG, October 30, 1753.

With these instructions Washington proceeded to the Ohio, to demand the withdrawal of the French from the soil claimed as English territory. This act opened a series of struggles, in the course of which English, French, and Americans, changed their relative positions, and which closed thirty years after, with the gaze of mankind riveted on the august form of him, whom we here behold the stripling.

By that series of struggles America alone profited. The mighty Genius directing her destiny seems to have used the power of England to drive France from the north and west and south, and then used baffled France to drive the English power within that line of lakes which Dongan, a century before, marked as our boundary; used France, too, at a later day, to add to the American limits, that Louisiana which she could not hold herself, so that ere the century succeeding the events here described had reached its close, a mighty republic, stretching from the Atlantic to the Pacific, reveres, perpetuates, and exalts the name of Washington.

J. G. S.

ADVERTISEMENT.

As it was thought advisable by his Honour the Governor, to have the following account of my proceedings to and from the French on the Ohio committed to print, I think I can do no less than apologize, in some measure, for the numberless imperfections of it. There intervened but one day between my arrival in Williamsburg and the time for the Council's meeting, for me to prepare and transcribe, from the rough minutes I had taken in my travels, this journal; the writing of which only was sufficient to employ me closely the whole time, consequently admitted of no leisure to consult of a new and proper form to offer it in, or to correct and amend the diction of the old; neither was I apprised, nor did in the least conceive, when I wrote this for his Honour's perusal, that it ever would be published, or even have more than a cursory reading; till I was informed, at the meeting of the present General Assembly, that it was already in the press. There is nothing can recommend it to the public but this: those things which came under the notice of my own observation, I have been explicit and just in a recital of; those which I have gathered from report, I have been particularly cautious not to augment, but collected the opinions of the several intelligencers, and selected from the whole the most probable and consistent account.

G. WASHINGTON.

OCTOBER 31st, 1753.

I was commissioned and appointed by the Hon. Robert Dinwiddie, Esq., Governor of Virginia,[1] to visit and deliver a letter to the commandant of the French forces on the Ohio, and set out on the intended journey on the same day (October 31, 1753); the next, I arrived at Fredericksburg, and engaged Mr. Jacob Vanbraam[2] to be my French interpreter, and proceeded with him to Alexandria, where we provided necessaries. From thence we went to Winchester, and got baggage, horses, &c., and from thence we pursued the new road to Will's Creek, where we arrived on the 14th of November.

---

[1] Robert Dinwiddie, a native of Scotland, had been a clerk to a collector in a West-India custom-house, and gained the favor of government, by exposing the frauds of that officer. For this he was, in 1741, made surveyor of the customs of the Colonies, and having in that capacity been obnoxious to the Virginia aristocracy, was made lieutenant-governor of Virginia in 1752. His administration was like that of most colonial governors. Campbell thus describes its close, in his "History of Virginia," p. 497: "In January, 1758, Robert Dinwiddie, after an arduous and disturbed administration of five years, worn out with vexation and age, sailed from Virginia, not much regretted, except by his particular friends."

[2] Jacob Van Braam had served under Lawrence Washington, in Vernon's expedition against Carthagena, and had been fencing-master, as he was now interpreter, to George Washington. In the subsequent campaign when Washington capitulated at Fort Necessity, Van Braam, acting as translator, made Washington admit that he had assassinated De Jumonville. After that affair, he was left, with Stobo, as hostage in the hands of the French.

Here I engaged Mr. Gist[3] to pilot us out, and also hired four others as servitors, Barnaby Currin, and John M'Quire, Indian traders, Henry Steward, and William Jenkins; and in company with those persons, left the inhabitants the next day.

NOVEMBER 22d.

The excessive rains and vast quantity of snow which had fallen prevented our reaching Mr. Frazier's, an Indian trader, at the mouth of Turtle Creek, on Monongahela River, until Thursday, the 22nd. We were informed here that expresses had been sent a few days before to the traders down the river, to acquaint them with the French general's death,[4] and the return of the major part of the French army into winter-quarters.

---

[3] Christopher Gist was an early settler in those parts, and Washington, in recommending his appointment as Indian agent, thus writes to John Robinson, speaker of the House of Burgesses, May 30, 1757 : "I know of no person so well qualified for an undertaking of this sort as the bearer, Captain Gist. He has had extensive dealings with the Indians, is in great esteem among them, well acquainted with their manners and customs, indefatigable and patient—most excellent qualities where Indians are concerned. As to his capacity, honesty, and zeal, I dare venture to engage."— *Writings*, vol. ii., p. 236.

[4] This French General was Pierre Paul, Sieur de Marin, a brave and intelligent officer, one of the best in Du Quesne's force, and high in the esteem of that reformer of discipline. Du Quesne had dispatched him to the Ohio, to found the fort at the confluence of the Alleghany and Monongahela. The register of Fort Duquesne has the following entry : "In the year one thousand seven hundred and fifty-three, the 29th of October, died at half-past four o'clock in the afternoon, in the Fort of Rivière aux Bœufs, under the title of St. Peter, Monsieur Pierre Paul, Esq., Sieur de Marin, Knight of the Military and Royal Order of St.

The waters were quite impassable without swimming our horses, which obliged us to get the loan of a canoe from Frazier, and to send Barnaby Currin and Henry Steward down the Monongahela, with our baggage, to meet us at the Fork of the Ohio, about ten miles ; there to cross the Allegany.

As I got down before the canoe, I spent some time in viewing the rivers, and the land in the Fork, which I think extremely well situated for a fort, as it has the absolute command of both rivers.[5] The land at the point is twenty,

---

Louis, Captain of Infantry and Commandant General of the army of the Ohio, after having received the sacraments of penance, extreme unction, and the viaticum, aged sixty-three years. His body was interred in the cemetery of said fort by us, Recollect priest, chaplain of said fort and, during the campaign, of the River Ohio. Were present at his interment, Monsieur de Repentigny, commandant of said army and captain of infantry, Messieurs, du Muys, lieutenant of infantry, Benois, lieutenant of infantry, de Simblin, major at said fort, Laforce, commissary of the stores, who have signed with us

"LE GARDEUR DE REPENTIGNY,
"LAFORCE—BENOIS—DU MUYS,
"J. DEPRÉ SIMBLIN,
"FRIAR DENIS BARON,
Recollect priest, chaplain."

Marin had just erected Forts Presque Isle and Le Bœuf. Du Quesne in his letter to M. De Rouille, August 20, 1753, says : "Sieur Marin writes me on the 3d inst. that the fort at Presque Isle is entirely finished ; that the Portage road, which is six leagues in length, is also ready for carriages ; that the store which was necessary to be built halfway across the Portage is in a condition to receive the supplies ; and that the second fort, which is located at the mouth of the Rivière au Bœuf, will soon be completed."—*N. Y. Col. Doc.*, x., 256.

[5] This choice, says Dussieux, proves the accurate glance and excellent judgment of the young major. But at the moment of his making

or twenty-five feet above the common surface of the water; and a considerable bottom of flat, well-timbered land all around it, very convenient for building. The rivers are each a quarter of a mile or more across, and run here very nearly at right angles, Allegany bearing northeast, and Monongahela southeast. The former of these two is a very rapid and swift running water, the other deep and still, without any perceptible fall.

About two miles from this, on the southeast side of the river, at the place where the Ohio Company intended to erect a fort, lives Shingiss, King of the Delawares.[6] We called upon him, to invite him to counsel at the Logstown.

As I had taken a good deal of notice yesterday of the situation at the Fork, my curiosity led me to examine this more particularly, and I think it greatly inferior, either for defence or advantages; especially the latter. For a fort at the Fork would be equally well situated on the Ohio, and have the entire command of the Monongahela, which runs up our settlement, and is extremely well designed for water-carriage, and it is of a deep, still nature. Besides, a fort at the Fork might be built at much less expense than at the other places.

Nature has well contrived this lower place for water-defence; but the hill whereon it must stand, being about a quarter of a mile in length, and then descending gradually on the land side, will render it difficult and very expen-

---

the report, the French were already erecting Fort Duquesne on the spot.—*Le Canada sous la Domination Française*, p. 61.

[6] Shingiss had been the terror of the English frontiers, but had now warmly espoused the cause of the English.

sive to make a sufficient fortification there. The whole flat upon the hill must be taken in, the side next the descent made extremely high, or else the hill itself cut away; otherwise the enemy may raise batteries within that distance without being exposed to a single shot from the fort.

Shingiss attended us to the Logstown, where we arrived between sun-setting and dark, the twenty-fifth day after I left Williamsburg. We travelled over some extremely good and bad land to get to this place.

As soon as I came into town, I went to Monacatoocha (as the Half-King[7] was out at his hunting cabin on Little Beaver Creek, about fifteen miles off), and informed him by John Davidson, my Indian interpreter, that I was sent a messenger to the French general, and was ordered to call upon the sachems of the Six Nations to acquaint them with it. I gave him a string of wampum and a twist of tobacco, and desired him to send for the Half-King, which he promised to do by a runner in the morning, and for other sachems. I invited him and the other great men present to my tent, where they stayed about an hour, and returned.

According to the best observations I could make, Mr. Gist's new settlement (which we passed by) bears about west northwest seventy miles from Will's Creek; Shannopins, or the Fork, north by west, or north northwest, about fifty miles from that; and from thence to the Logstown the course is nearly west about eighteen or twenty miles; so

---

[7] Half-King. Tanacharisson, a shrewd Seneca, was called the Half-King, as his authority was subject to that of the Five Nations. Campbell's "History of Virginia," p. 461. Sargent's "Braddock," p. 54. He was with Washington in the affair with Jumonville, and died in Oct. 1754.

that the whole distance, as we went and computed it, is at least one hundred and thirty-five, or one hundred and forty miles from our back inhabitants.

NOVEMBER 25th.

Came to town, four of ten Frenchmen, who had deserted from a company at the Kuskuskas,[8] which lies at the mouth of this river. I got the following account from them. They were sent from New Orleans with a hundred men, and eight canoe loads of provisions to this place, where they expected to have met the same number of men, from the forts on this side of Lake Erie, to convoy them and the stores up, who were not arrived when they ran off.

I inquired into the situation of the French on the Mississippi, their numbers, and what forts they had built. They informed me that there were four small forts between New Orleans and the Black Islands,[9] garrisoned with about thirty or forty men, and a few small pieces in each. That at New Orleans, which is near the mouth of the Mississippi, there are thirty-five companies of forty men each, with a pretty strong fort mounting eight carriage guns; and at the Black Islands there are several companies, and a fort with six guns. The Black Islands are about a hundred and thirty

---

[8] Kuskuskas was, it is said, an Indian town on Big Beaver Creek, Pennsylvania.

[9] Black Islands. Washington was here evidently misled by the sound, and mistook Illinois for Isles Noires, that is Black Islands. There was no French post called Black Islands, but the name Illinois, now so familiar to us, was then unheard in the British colonies. The Miamis and Illinois were known as Chicktaghicks and Twigtwies, and both together frequently under the last, the more common term.

leagues above the mouth of the Ohio, which is about three hundred and fifty above New Orleans. They also acquainted me that there was a small palisadoed fort on the Ohio, at the mouth of the Obaish,[10] about sixty leagues from the Mississippi. The Obaish heads near the west end of Lake Erie, and affords the communication between the French on the Mississippi and those on the lakes. These deserters came up from the lower Shannoah[11] town with one Brown, an Indian trader, and were going to Philadelphia.

About three o'clock this evening, the Half-King came to town. I went up and invited him, with Davidson, privately, to my tent, and desired him to relate some of the particulars of his journey to the French commandant, and of his reception there; also, to give me an account of the ways and distance. He told me that the nearest and levelest way was now impassable, by reason of many large, miry savannas; that we must be obliged to go by Venango,[12] and

---

[10] Obaish, Wabash; in French, Ouabache. This name was given by Marquette, La Salle, and other early explorers, to the Ohio, but finally became that of a branch, while the Iroquois name, Ohio, or Beautiful River, was applied to the main stream. The fort alluded to was probably Vincennes.

[11] Shawanoe, or, as now written, Shawnee. They were called by the French, Chawanon. They were the most restless of the Algonquin tribes, having been for a longer or shorter period in almost all the Atlantic colonies, from Florida to New York, and bands of them accompanied La Salle and Tonti up and down the Mississippi, one of them even sharing the death of the great explorer.

[12] Venango. Fort Venango was at the confluence of French Creek and the Alleghany, on the left; and another French fort, Machault, lay on the right. The ruins of Fort Venango cover a space of about four hundred feet, and the ramparts are eight feet high.

should not get to the near fort in less than five or six night's sleep, good travelling. When he went to the fort, he said he was received in a very stern manner by the late commander, who asked him very abruptly what he had come about, and to declare his business, which he said he did in the following speech :—

"Fathers, I am come to tell you your own speeches, what your own mouths have declared.

"Fathers, you, in former days, set a silver basin before us, wherein there was the leg of a beaver, and desired all the nations to come and eat of it, to eat in peace and plenty, and not to be churlish to one another ; and that if any such person should be found to be a disturber, I here lay down by the edge of the dish a rod, which you must scourge them with ; and if your father should get foolish, in my old days, I desire you may use it upon me as well as others.

"Now, fathers, it is you who are the disturbers in this land, by coming and building your towns, and taking it away unknown to us, and by force.

"Fathers, we kindled a fire a long time ago at a place called Montreal, where we desired you to stay, and not to come and intrude upon our land. I now desire you may dispatch to that place ; for be it known to you, fathers, that this is our land, and not yours.

"Fathers, I desire you may hear me in civilness ; if not, we must handle that rod which was laid down for the use of the obstreperous. If you had come in a peaceable manner, like our brothers the English, we would not have been against your trading with us as they do ; but to come, fathers, and build houses upon our land, and to take it by force, is what we cannot submit to.

"Fathers, both you and the English are white, we live in a country between; therefore, the land belongs to neither one nor the other. But the Great Being above allowed it to be a place of residence for us; so, fathers, I desire you to withdraw, as I have done our brothers the English; for I will keep you at arm's length. I lay this down as a trial for both, to see which will have the greatest regard to it, and that side we will stand by, and make equal sharers with us. Our brothers, the English, have heard this, and I come now to tell it to you; for I am not afraid to discharge you off this land."

This, he said, was the substance of what he spoke to the general, who made this reply:—

" Now, my child, I have heard your speech; you spoke first, but it is my time to speak now. Where is my wampum that you took away with the marks of towns on it? This wampum I do not know, which you have discharged me off the land with; but you need not put yourself to the trouble of speaking, for I will not hear you. I am not afraid of flies or musquitoes, for Indians are such as those; I tell you down that river I will go, and build upon it, according to my command. If the river was blocked up, I have forces sufficient to burst it open, and tread under my feet all that stand in opposition, together with their alliances; for my force is as the sand upon the sea shore; therefore, here is your wampum; I sling it at you. Child, you talk foolish; you say this land belongs to you, but there is not the black of my nail yours. I saw that land sooner

than you did; before the Shannoahs and you were at war.
Lead was the man who went down and took possession of
that river. It is my land, and I will have it, let who will
stand up for, or say against it. I will buy and sell with the
English (mockingly.) If people will be ruled by me, they
may expect kindness, but not else."

The Half-King told me he had inquired of the general
after two Englishmen who were made prisoners, and received this answer :—

"Child, you think it a very great hardship that I made
prisoners of those two people at Venango. Don't you concern yourself with it; we took and carried them to Canada,
to get intelligence of what the English were doing in Virginia."

He informed me that they had built two forts, one on
Lake Erie,[13] and another on French Creek, near a small
lake,[14] about fifteen miles asunder, and a large wagon-road
between. They are both built after the same model, but
different in size; that on the lake the largest. He gave
me a plan of them of his own drawing.

The Indians inquired very particularly after their brothers in Carolina gaol.

They also asked what sort of a boy it was who was taken
from the South Branch; for they were told by some Indians

---

[13] Fort Presque Isle, lay near the site of the present Erie, and extensive earthworks can still be seen.

[14] Fort Le Bœuf, or Fort de la Rivière aux Bœufs. See Washington's
description of it under date of December 13th. It stood on the banks
of Lake Le Bœuf, about fourteen miles southeast of Erie, near the present village of Waterford, where its ruins are still to be seen.

that a party of French Indians had carried a white boy by Kuskuska Town, towards the lakes.

November 26th.

We met in council at the long-house about nine o'clock, where I spoke to them as follows :—

"Brothers, I have called you together in council, by order of your brother, the Governor of Virginia, to acquaint you that I am sent with all possible dispatch to visit and deliver a letter to the French commandant of very great importance to your brothers the English ; and I dare say to you, their friends and allies.

"I was desired, brothers, by your brother, the Governor, to call upon you, the sachems of the nations, to inform you of it, and to ask your advice and assistance to proceed the nearest and best road to the French. You see, brothers, I have gotten thus far on my journey.

"His Honour likewise desired me to apply to you for some of your young men to conduct and provide provisions for us on our way, and be a safeguard against those French Indians who have taken up the hatchet against us. I have spoken thus particularly to you, brothers, because his Honour, our Governor, treats you as good friends and allies, and holds you in great esteem. To confirm what I have said, I give you this string of wampum."

After they had considered for some time on the above discourse, the Half-King got up and spoke :—

"Now, my brother, in regard to what my brother the Governor had desired of me, I return you this answer :—

"I rely upon you as a brother ought to do, as you say we

are brothers, and one people. We shall put heart in hand and speak to our fathers, the French, concerning the speech they made to me; and you may depend that we will endeavour to be your guard.

"Brother, as you have asked my advice, I hope you will be ruled by it, and stay until I can provide a company to go with you. The French speech-belt is not here; I have to go for it to my hunting-cabin. Likewise, the people whom I have ordered in are not yet come, and cannot until the third night from this; until which time, brother, I must beg you to stay.

"I intend to send the guard of Mingoes,[15] Shannoahs, and Delawares,[16] that our brothers may see the love and loyalty we bear them."

---

[15] Mingoes. The Mengwe, Minquas, or Mingoes, were properly the Andastes or Gandastogues, the Indians of Conestoga, on the Susquehanna, known by the former name to the Algonquins, and their allies, the Dutch and Swedes, and by the former to the Five Nations and the English of New York. The Marylanders knew them as the Susquehannas. Upon their reduction by the Five Nations in 1672 after a long war, the Andastes were to a great extent mingled with their conquerors, and a party removing to the Ohio, commonly called Mingoes, was thus made up, of Iroquois and Mingoes. The celebrated Logan was a real Andaste. Many treat Mingo as synonymous with Mohawk or Iroquois, but erroneously.

[16] Delawares. This well-known tribe was a small Algonquin nation, calling itself Lenni Lenape. They were early subdued by the Five Nations, and seemed to have acquired the considerable historic place they occupy more from the fertility of their traditionary mind than from important deeds in war or peace. In our earlier histories they assume gigantic importance, and their migrations and wars are detailed at length. These are, however, very doubtful. That they are a branch of the Illinois, emigrating to the east, seems probable.

As I had orders to make all possible dispatch, and waiting here was very contrary to my inclination, I thanked him in the most suitable manner I could, and told him that my business required the greatest expedition, and would not admit of that delay. He was not well pleased that I should offer to go before the time he had appointed, and told me that he could not consent to our going without a guard, for fear some accident should befall us, and draw a reflection upon him. Besides, said he, this is a matter of no small moment, and must not be entered into without due consideration; for I intend to deliver up the French speech-belt, and make the Shannoahs and Delawares do the same. And accordingly he gave orders to King Shingiss, who was present, to attend on Wednesday night with the wampum; and two men of their nation to be in readiness to set out with us the next morning. As I found it was impossible to get off without affronting them in the most egregious manner, I consented to stay.

I gave them back a string of wampum which I met with at Mr. Frazier's, and which they sent with a speech to his Honour the Governor, to inform him that three nations of French Indians,—namely, Chippewas,[17] Ottawas,[18] and Orun-

[17] The Chippewas were first known to the French, as Otchiboués, answering to the modern form Ojibwa, or Otchipwe. They are an Algonquin tribe, whose residence was at Sault Ste. Marie, whence the later French called them Sauteux, men of the Sault. Their language, traditions, and customs, have been more thoroughly studied than those of any other of our Indian tribes.

[18] The Ottawas were another Algonquin tribe found on Lake Ontario. They formed, when first known, two branches, the Kiskakons and Sinagoes, and were remarkably errant. Their fires were lighted at

daks,[19] had taken up the hatchet against the English; and
desired them to repeat it over again. But this they postponed doing until they met in full council with the Shannoah and Delaware chiefs.

NOVEMBER 27th.

Runners were dispatched very early for the Shannoah
chiefs. The Half-King set out himself to fetch the French
speech-belt from his hunting-cabin.

NOVEMBER 28th.

He returned this evening, and came with Monacatoocha
and two other sachems to my tent, and begged (as they had
complied with his Honour the Governor's request, in providing men, &c.) to know on what business we were going
to the French. This was a question I had all along expected, and had provided as satisfactory answers as I could;
which allayed their curiosity a little.

Monacatoocha informed me that an Indian from Venango brought news a few days ago that the French had

---

different times from Chagoimegon to Detroit. They are now chiefly
on the eastern shore of Lake Michigan. Their language bears a very
close resemblance to the Ojibwa.

[19] The Orundaks are evidently the Adirondacks of New York writers,
the Algonquin of the French. Adirondack is a Mohawk term, mean-
ing, *they eat trees*, from karonta, *tree;* and iraks, *he eats*. A small village
of them still exists at the Lake of the Two Mountains, Canada East.
They were hereditary enemies of the Five Nations, and their alliance
with the Hurons drew the latter into a war, in which both were utter-
ly prostrated, by the great confederation of New York.

called all the Mingoes, Delawares, &c., together at that place; and told them that they intended to have been down the river this fall, but the waters were growing cold, and the winter advancing, which obliged them to go into quarters; but that they might assuredly expect them in the spring with a far greater number; and desired that they might be quite passive, and not intermeddle unless they had a mind to draw all their force upon them; for that they expected to fight the English three years (as they supposed there would be some attempts made to stop them), in which time they should conquer. But that if they should prove equally strong, they and the English would join to cut them all off, and divide the land between them; that though they had lost their general and some few of their soldiers, yet there were men enough to reinforce them, and make them masters of the Ohio.

This speech, he said, was delivered to them by one Captain Joncaire,[20] their interpreter-in-chief, living at Venango, and a man of note in the army.

---

[20] No name figures more extensively in our border history than the Sieur de Joncaire, father and son, of whom, however, comparatively little is known. The former had been a prisoner in the hands of the Senecas, and adopted by them as early as 1700, and in that year they asked that he should go to their canton to arrange terms of peace, which he did with success. In all subsequent transactions with the Iroquois he plays a conspicuous part, his Indian naturalization making it impossible for the English authorities to obtain his expulsion.—Charlevoix, *Hist. Nouvelle France*, ii., 244-365. He was apparently the first European who examined the oil springs recently rendered so profitable. His son, the Joncaire of this diary, continued his father's influence among the Senecas, till Shirley, when at Oswego, in 1755, induced them to order him to depart.—Smith's *New York* (ed. 1830), i., 275.

NOVEMBER 29th.

The Half-King and Monacatoocha came very early, and begged me to stay one day more ; for notwithstanding they had used all the diligence in their power, the Shannoah chiefs had not brought the wampum they ordered, but would certainly be in to-night; if not, they would delay me no longer, but would send it after us as soon as they arrived. When I found them so pressing in their request, and knew that the returning of wampum was the abolishing of agreements, and giving this up was shaking off all dependence upon the French, I consented to stay, as I believed an offence offered at this crisis might be attended with greater ill consequence than another day's delay. They also informed me that Shingiss could not get in his men, and was prevented from coming himself by his wife's sickness (I believe by fear of the French), but that the wampum of that nation was lodged with Kustalogo, one of their chiefs, at Venango.

In the evening, late, they came again, and acquainted me that the Shannoahs were not yet arrived, but that it should not retard the prosecution of our journey. He delivered in my hearing the speech that was to be made to the French by Jeskakake, one of their old chiefs, which was giving up the belt the late commandant had asked for, and repeating nearly the same speech he himself had done before.

He also delivered a string of wampum to this chief, which was sent by King Shingiss, to be given to Kustalogo, with orders to repair to the French, and deliver up the wampum.

He likewise gave a very large string of black and white wampum, which was to be sent up immediately to the Six Nations, if the French refused to quit the land at this warning, which was the third and last time, and was the right of this Jeskakake to deliver.

November 30th.

Last night, the great men assembled at their council house, to consult further about this journey, and who were to go; the result of which was, that only three of their chiefs, with one of their best hunters, should be our convoy. The reason they gave for not sending more, after what had been proposed at council the 26th, was, that a greater number might give the French suspicions of some bad design, and cause them to be treated rudely; but I rather think they could not get their hunters in.

We set out about nine o'clock with the Half-King, Jeskakake, White Thunder, and the Hunter; and travelled on the road to Venango, where we arrived the 4th of December, without anything remarkable happening but a continued series of bad weather.

This is an old Indian town, situated at the mouth of French Creek, on the Ohio; and lies near north about sixty miles from the Logstowu, but more than seventy the way we were obliged to go.

We found the French colours hoisted at a house from which they had driven Mr. John Frazier, an English subject. I immediately repaired to it, to know where the commander resided. There were three officers, one of whom, Captain Joncaire, informed me that he had the command of the Ohio ; but that there was a general officer at the near fort, where he advised me to apply for an answer. He invited us to sup with them, and treated us with the greatest complaisance.

The wine, as they dosed themselves pretty plentifully with it, soon banished the restraint which at first appeared in their conversation, and gave a licence to their tongues to reveal their sentiments more freely.

They told me that it was their absolute design to take possession of the Ohio, and by G— they would do it; for that, although they were sensible the English could raise two men for their one, yet they knew their motions were too slow and dilatory to prevent any undertaking of theirs. They pretend to have an undoubted right to the river from a discovery made by one La Salle,[21] sixty years ago; and the rise of this expedition is, to prevent our settling on the

---

[21] La Salle. Robert Cavelier de la Salle, it is known, followed up the discovery of Marquette and Joliet, and in 1682 descended the Mississippi to its mouth, which he reached on the 9th of April. He planted the arms of France, and took possession of the river and all the country watered by it and its branches. This extended the French claim to the head waters of the Alleghany and Monongahela. See " The Discovery and Exploration of the Mississippi," and narrative there given. Pierre de Margry, a recent French writer, asserts that in 1670–1, La Salle descended the Ohio to the Mississippi (Dussieux, Canada, p. 37); but the proof has not been given, and not improbably is a delusion, as no notice of the fact appears in any document of the time, and the friends of La Salle would not be likely to omit an expedition giving him a clear priority to the discovery of the Mississippi, nor would La Salle, having a post at Niagara, overlook the advantage of following the same course to reach the mouth of the Mississippi.

river or waters of it, as they heard of some families moving
out in order thereto. From the best intelligence I could
get, there have been fifteen hundred men on this side Ontario Lake. But upon the death of the general, all were
recalled, to about six or seven hundred, who were left to
garrison four forts, one hundred and fifty, or thereabout, in
each. The first of them is on French Creek,[22] near a small
lake, about sixty miles from Venango, near north north-
west; the next lies on Lake Erie,[23] where the greater part
of their stores are kept, about fifteen miles from the other;
from this it is one hundred and twenty miles to the carry-
ing-place, at the Falls of Lake Erie, where there is a small
fort,[24] at which they lodge their goods in bringing them
from Montreal, the place from whence all their stores are
brought. The next fort lies about twenty miles from this,
on Ontario Lake.[25] Between this fort and Montreal, there
are three others, the first of which[26] is nearly opposite to the
English fort Oswego. From the fort on Lake Erie to Montreal is about six hundred miles, which, they say, requires
no more (if good weather) than four weeks' voyage, if they
go in barks or large vessels, so that they may cross the
lake; but if they come in canoes, it will require five or six
weeks, for they are obliged to keep under the shore.

DECEMBER 5th.

Rained excessively all day, which prevented our travel-

---

[22] Fort Le Bœuf.   [23] Fort Presque Isle.   [24] Fort Niagara.
[25] Fort Toronto.   [26] Fort Frontenac.

ling. Captain Joncaire sent for the Half-King, as he had but just heard that he came with me. He affected to be much concerned that I did not make free to bring them in before. I excused it in the best manner of which I was capable, and told him, I did not think their company agreeable, as I had heard him say a good deal in dispraise of Indians in general; but another motive prevented me from bringing them into his company; I knew that he was an interpreter, and a person of very great influence among the Indians, and had lately used all possible means to draw them over to his interest; therefore I was desirous of giving him no opportunity that could be avoided.

When they came in there was great pleasure expressed at seeing them. He wondered how they could be so near without coming to visit him, made several trifling presents, and applied liquor so fast that they were soon rendered incapable of the business they came about, notwithstanding the caution which was given.[27]

DECEMBER 6th.

The Half-King came to my tent quite sober, and insisted very much that I should stay and hear what he had to say

---

[27] Gist, in his journal, here notes : " Our Indians were in council with the Delawares, who lived under the French colors, and ordered them to deliver up to the French the belt with the marks of the four towns, according to the desire of King Shingiss. But the chief of these Delawares said: ' It was true, King Shingiss was a great man, but he had sent no speech, and,' said he, ' I cannot pretend to make a speech for a king.' So our Indians could not prevail with them to deliver their belt ; but the Half-King did deliver his belt as he had determined."

to the French. I fain would have prevented him from speaking anything until he came to the commandant, but could not prevail. He told me that at this place a council fire was kindled, where all their business with these people was to be transacted, and that the management of the Indian affairs was left solely to Monsieur Joncaire. As I was desirous of knowing the issue of this, I agreed to stay; but sent our horses a little way up French Creek, to raft over and encamp, which I knew would make it near night.

About ten o'clock they met in council. The King spoke much the same as he had before done to the general; and offered the French speech-belt which had before been demanded, with the marks of four towns on it, which Monsieur Joncaire refused to receive, but desired him to carry it to the fort to the commander.

December 7th.

Monsieur La Force, commissary of the French stores, and three other soldiers, came over to accompany us up. We found it extremely difficult to get the Indians off to-day, as every stratagem had been used to prevent their going up with me. I had last night left John Davidson (the Indian interpreter), whom I had brought with me from town, and strictly charged him not to be out of their company, as I could not get them over to my tent; for they had some business with Kustalogo, chiefly to know why he did not deliver up the French speech-belt which he had in keeping; but I was obliged to send Mr. Gist over to-day to fetch them, which he did with great persuasion.

At twelve o clock, we set out for the fort, and were prevented arriving there until the 11th by excessive rains, snows, and bad travelling through many mires and swamps; these we were obliged to pass to avoid crossing the creek, which was impassable, either by fording or rafting, the water was so high and rapid.

We passed over much good land since we left Venango, and through several extensive and very rich meadows, one of which, I believe, was nearly four miles in length, and considerably wide in some places.

December 12th.

I prepared early to wait upon the commander, and was received and conducted to him by the second officer in command. I acquainted him with my business, and offered him my commission and letter; both of which he desired me to keep until the arrival of Monsieur Reparti, captain at the next fort, who was sent for and expected every hour.

This commander is a knight of the military order of St. Louis, and named Legardeur de St. Pierre.[28] He is an eld-

---

[28] Le Gardeur de St. Pierre. The family of Le Gardeur de Repentigny descended from Pierre Le Gardeur, Sieur de Repentigny, one of the earliest settlers near Quebec. Mr. Ferland, in his "Notes on the Register of Quebec," p. 53, remarks that members of this family, and that of Charles Le Gardeur de Tilly took part in every war of New France, from Louisiana to Acadia and Newfoundland. He adds, on p. 57, that both have completely disappeared from Canada. The officer who succeeded Marin signs in the Register, Le Gardeur de Repentigny, but in the letter to Dinwiddie, Le Gardeur de St Pierre, and is apparently the one known as M. de St. Pierre, who was killed at Bloody Pond. The younger one, styled M. de Repentigny, would seem, however, to be intended by the M. Reparti of Washington's Diary.

erly gentleman, and has much the air of a soldier. He was sent over to take the command immediately upon the death of the late general, and arrived here about seven days before me.

At two o'clock, the gentleman who was sent for arrived, when I offered the letter, &c., again, which they received, and adjourned into a private apartment for the captain to translate, who understood a little English. After he had done it, the commander desired I would walk in and bring my interpreter to peruse and correct it; which I did.

December 13th.

The chief officers retired to hold a council of war, which gave me an opportunity of taking the dimensions of the fort, and making what observations I could.

It is situated on the south or west fork of French Creek, near the water; and is almost surrounded by the creek, and a small branch of it, which form a kind of island. Four houses compose the sides. The bastions are made of piles driven into the ground, standing more than twelve feet above it, and sharp at top, with port-holes cut for cannon, and loop-holes for the small arms to fire through. There are eight six-pounds pieces mounted in each bastion, and one piece of four pounds before the gate. In the bastions are a guard-house, chapel, doctor's lodging, and the commander's private store; round which are laid platforms for the cannon and men to stand on. There are several barracks without the fort, for the soldiers' dwellings, covered, some with bark and some with boards made chiefly of logs.

There are also several other houses, such as stables, smith's shop, &c.

I could get no certain account of the number of men here ; but, according to the best judgment I could form, there are a hundred, exclusive of officers, of whom there are many. I also gave orders to the people who were with me to take an exact account of the canoes, which were hauled up to convey their forces down in the spring. This they did, and told fifty of birch bark, and a hundred and seventy of pine, besides many others, which were blocked out, in readiness for being made.

December 14th.

As the snow increased very fast, and our horses daily became weaker, I sent them off unloaded, under the care of Barnaby Currin and two others, to make all convenient dispatch to Venango, and there to wait our arrival, if there was a prospect of the river's freezing ; if not, then to continue down to Shannopin's Town, at the Fork of the Ohio, and there to wait until we came to cross the Allegany, intending myself to go down by water, as I had the offer of a canoe or two.

As I found many plots concerted to retard the Indians' business, and prevent their returning with me, I endeavoured all that lay in my power to frus rate their schemes, and hurried them on to execute their intended design. They accordingly pressed for admittance this evening, which at length was granted them, privately, to the commander and one or two other officers. The Half-King told me that he offered the wampum to the commander, who evaded taking it, and made many fair promises of love and friendship; said he wanted to live in peace, and trade amicably with them, as a proof of which, he would send some goods immediately down to the Logstown for them. But I rather think the design of that is to bring away all our straggling traders they meet with, as I privately understood they intended to carry an officer with them. And what rather confirms this opinion, I was inquiring of the commander by what authority he had made prisoners of several of our English subjects. He told me that the country belonged to them; that no Englishman had a right to trade upon those waters; and that he had orders to make every person prisoner who attempted it on the Ohio, or the waters of it.

I inquired of Captain Reparti about the boy that was carried by this place, as it was done while the command devolved on him, between the death of the late general and the arrival of the present. He acknowledged that a boy had been carried past; and that the Indians had two or three white men's scalps, (I was told by some of the Indians at Venango, eight,) but pretended to have forgotten the name of the place where the boy came from, and all the particular facts, though he had questioned him for some hours as they were carrying him past. I likewise inquired what they had done with John Trotter and James M'Clocklan, two Pennsylvania traders, whom they had taken with all their goods. They told me that they had been sent to Canada, but were now returned home.

This evening I received an answer to his Honour the Governor's letter from the commandant.

December 15th.

The commandant ordered a plentiful store of liquor and provision to be put on board our canoes, and appeared to be extremely complaisant, though he was exerting every artifice which he could invent to set our Indians at variance with us, to prevent their going until after our departure; presents, rewards, and everything which could be suggested by him or his officers. I cannot say that ever in my life I suffered so much anxiety as I did in this affair. I saw that every stratagem which the most fruitful brain could invent was practised to win the Half-King to their interest; and that leaving him there was giving them the opportunity they aimed at. I went to the Half-King and pressed him in the strongest terms to go; he told me that the commandant would not discharge him until the morning. I then went to the commandant, and desired him to do their business, and complained of ill treatment; for keeping them, as they were part of my company, was detaining me. This he promised not to do, but to forward my journey as much as he could. He protested he did not keep them, but was ignorant of the cause of their stay; though I soon found it out. He had promised them a present of guns, if they would wait until the morning. As I was very much pressed by the Indians to wait this day for them, I consented, on a promise that nothing should hinder them in the morning.

December 16th.

The French were not slack in their inventions to keep the Indians this day also. But as they were obliged, according to promise, to give the present, they then endeavoured to try the power of liquor, which I doubt not would have prevailed at any other time than this; but I urged and insisted with the King so closely upon his word that he refrained, and set off with us as he had engaged.

We had a tedious and very fatiguing passage down the creek. Several times we had liked to have been staved against rocks; and many times were obliged all hands to get out and remain in the water half an hour or more, getting over the shoals. At one place, the ice had lodged and made it impassable by water; we were therefore obliged to carry our canoe across the neck of land, a quarter of a mile over. We did not reach Venango until the 22nd, where we met with our horses.

This creek is extremely crooked. I dare say the distance between the fort and Venango cannot be less than one hundred and thirty miles, to follow the meanders.

December 23d.

When I got things ready to set off, I sent for the Half-King to know whether he intended to go with us or by water. He told me that White Thunder had hurt himself much, and was sick and unable to walk; therefore he was obliged to carry him down in a canoe. As I found he intended to stay here a day or two, and knew that Monsieur Joncaire would employ every scheme to set him against the English, as he had before done, I told him I hoped he would guard against his flattery, and let no fine speeches influence him in their favour. He desired I might not be concerned, for he knew the French too well for anything to engage him in their favour; and that though he could not go down with us, he yet would endeavour to meet at the Fork with Joseph Campbell, to deliver a speech for me to carry to his Honour the Governor. He told me he would order the Young Hunter to attend us, and get provisions, &c., if wanted.

Our horses were now so weak and feeble, and the baggage so heavy (as we were obliged to provide all the necessaries which the journey would require), that we doubted much their performing it. Therefore, myself and others, except the drivers, who were obliged to ride, gave up our horses for packs, to assist along with the baggage. I put myself in an Indian walking-dress, and continued with them three days, until I found there was no probability of their getting home in any reasonable time. The horses became less able to travel every day; the cold increased very fast; and the roads were becoming much worse by a deep snow, continually freezing; therefore, as I was uneasy to get back, to make report of my proceedings to his Honour the Governor, I determined to prosecute my journey the nearest way through the woods on foot.

Accordingly, I left Mr. Vanbraam in charge of our baggage, with money and directions to provide necessaries from place to place for themselves and horses, and to make the most convenient dispatch in travelling.

DECEMBER 26th.

I took my necessary papers, pulled off my clothes, and tied myself up in a watch-coat. Then, with gun in hand and pack on my back, in which were my papers and provisions, I set out with Mr. Gist, fitted in the same manner, on Wednesday, the 26th.[29] The day following, just after

---

[29] Gist opposed Washington's attempting this journey on foot, and his journal here being more full and explicit as to his Washington's sufferings than his own Diary, an extract will not be uninteresting: " I was unwilling he should undertake such a travel, who had never been used to walking before this time. But as he insisted on it, we set out with our packs, like Indians, and travelled eighteen miles. That night we lodged at an Indian cabin, and the major was much fatigued. It was very cold. All the small runs were frozen, so that we could hardly get water to drink.

" *Thursday*, 27th.—We rose early in the morning, and set out about two o'clock. Got to Murdering Town, on the southeast Fork of Beaver Creek. Here we met with an Indian, whom I thought I had seen at Joncaire's, at Venango, when on our journey up to the French fort. This fellow called me by my Indian name, and pretended to be glad to see me. He asked us several questions, as, how we came to travel on foot, when we left Venango, where we parted with our horses, and when they would be there. Major Washington insisted on travelling the nearest way to the forks of the Alleghany. We asked the Indian if he could go with us, and show us the nearest way. The Indian seemed very glad and ready to go with us. Upon which, we set out, and the Indian took the major's pack. We travelled very briskly for eight or ten miles, when the major's feet grew sore, and he very weary ; and the Indian steered too much northeastwardly.

"The major desired to encamp, on which the Indian asked to carry his gun. But he refused that, and then the Indian grew churlish, and

we had passed a place called Murdering Town (where we intended to quit the path and steer across the country for Shannopin's Town), we fell in with a party of French Indians, who had lain in wait for us. One of them fired at Mr. Gist or me, not fifteen steps off, but fortunately missed.

---

pressed us to keep on, telling us that there were Ottawa Indians in these woods, and that they would scalp us if we lay out; but to go to his cabin, and we should be safe. I thought very ill of the fellow, but did not care to let the major know I mistrusted him. But soon he mistrusted him as much as I. He said he could hear a gun to his cabin, and steered us more northwardly. We grew uneasy; and then he said that two whoops might be heard to his cabin. We went two miles further. Then the major said he would stay at the next water, and we desired the Indian to stop at the next water. But before we came to water, we came to a clear meadow. It was very light and there was snow on the ground. The Indian made a stop and turned about. The major saw him point his gun towards us and fire. Said the major 'Are you shot?' 'No,' said I. Upon this, the Indian ran forward to a big standing white oak, and went to loading his gun; but we were soon with him. I would have killed him, but the major would not suffer me to kill him.

"We let him charge his gun. We found he put in a ball. Then we took care of him. The major or I always stood by the guns. We made the Indian make a fire for us by a little run, as if we intended to sleep there. I said to the major, 'As you will not have him killed we must get him away, and then we must travel all night.' Upon this I said to the Indian, 'I suppose you were lost and fired your gun.' He said he knew the way to his cabin, and that it was but a little way. 'Well,' said I, 'do you go home; and as we are much tired, we will follow your track in the morning; and here is a cake of bread for you, and you must give us meat in the morning.' He was glad to get away. I followed him, and listened until he was fairly out of the way. Then we set out about half a mile, when we made a fire, set our compass and fixed our course, and travelled all night. In the morning we were at the head of Piney Creek."

We took this fellow into custody, and kept him till about nine o'clock at night, then let him go, and walked all the remaining part of the night without making any stop, that we might get the start so far as to be out of the reach of their pursuit the next day, since we were well assured they would follow our track as soon as it was light. The next day we continued travelling until quite dark, and got to the river about two miles above Shannopin's. We expected to have found the river frozen, but it was not, only about fifty yards from each shore. The ice, I suppose, had broken up above, for it was driving in vast quantities.

There was no way for getting over but on a raft, which we set about with but one poor hatchet, and finished just after sun-setting. This was a whole day's work; we next got it launched, then went on board of it and set off; but before we were half way over, we were jammed in the ice in such a manner that we expected every moment our raft to sink, and ourselves to perish. I put out my setting-pole to try to stop the raft, that the ice might pass by, when the rapidity of the stream threw it with so much violence against the pole that it jerked me out into ten feet water; but I fortunately saved myself by catching hold of one of the raft-logs. Notwithstanding all our efforts, we could not get to either shore, but were obliged, as we were near an island, to quit our raft and make to it.

The cold was so extremely severe that Mr. Gist had all his fingers and some of his toes frozen; and the water was shut up so hard that we found no difficulty in getting off the island on the ice in the morning, and went to Mr. Frazier's. We met here with twenty warriors, who were going to the southward to war; but coming to a place on the head Great Kenhawa, where they found seven people killed and scalped (all but one woman with very light hair), they turned about and ran back, for fear the inhabitants should rise and take them as the authors of the murder. They report that the bodies were lying about the house, and some of them much torn and eaten by the hogs. By the marks which were left, they say, they were French Indians of the Ottoway nation who did it.

As we intended to take horses here, and it required some time to find them, I went up about three miles to the mouth of Youghiogany, to visit Queen Aliquippa, who had expressed great concern that we passed her in going to the fort. I made her a present of a watch-coat and a bottle of rum, which latter was thought much the better present of the two.

TUESDAY, the 1st of JANUARY.

We left Mr. Frazier's house, and arrived at Mr. Gist's, at Monongahela,[30] the 2nd, where I bought a horse and saddle. The 6th, we met seventeen horses loaded with materials and stores for a fort at the Fork of the Ohio, and the day after, some families going out to settle. This day we arrived at Will's Creek, after as fatiguing a journey as it is possible to conceive, rendered so by excessive bad weather.

---

[30] Monongahela, said to be from the Shawnee Mehmonawangehelak, Falling-in-bank-river. Alleghany, the name of the other branch of the Ohio, is Iroquois, and signifies Cold-water.

From the 1st day of December to the 15th, there was but one day on which it did not rain or snow incessantly ; and throughout the whole journey we met with nothing but one continued series of cold, wet weather, which occasioned very uncomfortable lodgings, especially after we had quitted our tent, which was some screen from the inclemency of it.

On the 11th, I got to Belvoir, where I stopped one day to take necessary rest, and then set out and arrived in Williamsburg the 16th, when I waited upon his Honour the Governor, with the letter I had brought from the French commandant, and to give an account of the success of my proceedings. This I beg leave to do by offering the foregoing narrative, as it contains the most remarkable occurrences which happened in my journey.

I hope what has been said will be sufficient to make your Honour satisfied with my conduct, for that was my aim in undertaking the journey, and chief study throughout the prosecution of it.

LETTER OF GOVERNOR DINWIDDIE OF VIRGINIA TO THE
FRENCH COMMANDANT ON THE OHIO.

SIR:—The lands upon the river Ohio, in the western
parts of the Colony of Virginia, are so notoriously known
to be the property of the Crown of Great Britain, that it is
a matter of equal concern and surprise to me to hear that
a body of French forces are erecting fortresses and making
settlements upon that river, within his Majesty's dominions.
The *many* and *repeated* complaints I have received of these
acts of *hostility*, lay me under the necessity of sending, in
the name of the king, my master, the bearer hereof, George
Washington, Esq., one of the adjutants-general of the forces
of this dominion; to complain to you of the encroachments
thus made, and of the injuries done to the subjects of Great
Britain, in violation of the law of nations, and the treaties
now subsisting between the two crowns. If these facts be
true, and you think fit to justify your proceedings, I must
desire you to acquaint me by whose authority and instructions, you have lately marched from Canada with an armed
force, and invaded the King of Great Britain's territories,
in the manner complained of; that according to the purpose and resolution of your answer, I may act agreeably to
the commission I am honored with, from the king my master. However, Sir, in obedience to my instructions, it be-
comes my duty to require your peaceable departure; and

that you will forbear prosecuting a purpose so interruptive of the harmony and good understanding which his Majesty is desirous to continue and cultivate with the most Christian king, &c.

ROBERT DINWIDDIE.

———♦———

REPLY OF LE GARDEUR DE ST. PIERRE DE REPENTIGNY, COMMANDER OF THE FRENCH FORCES ON THE OHIO, TO GOVERNOR DINWIDDIE OF VIRGINIA.

SIR :—As I have the honor of commanding here in chief, Mr. Washington delivered to me the letter which you wrote to the commander of the French troops. I should have been glad, that you had given him orders, or that he had been inclined, to proceed to Canada to see our general; to whom it better belongs than to me, to set forth the evidence and the reality of the rights of the King, my master, to the lands situated along the River Ohio, and to contest the pretensions of the king of Great Britain thereto. I shall transmit your letter to the Marquis Du Quesne. His answer will be a law to me. And if he shall order me to communicate it to you, Sir, you may be assured, I shall not fail to dispatch it forthwith to you. As to the summons you send me to retire; I do not think myself obliged to obey it. Whatever may be your instructions, I am here by virtue of the orders of my general; and, I entreat you, Sir, not to doubt one moment, but that I am determined to con form myself to them with all the exactness and resolution which can be expected from the best officer. I do not know that in the progress of this campaign, any thing has passed, which can be reputed an act of hostility, or that is contrary to the treaties which subsist between the two crowns; the continuation whereof as much interesteth, and is as pleasing to us, as to the English. Had you been pleased, Sir, to have descended to particularize the facts, which occasioned your complaint, I should have had the honor of answering you in the fullest, and, I am persuaded, in the most satisfactory manner, &c.

LE GARDEUR DE ST. PIERRE.

From the Fort sur la Rivière au Bœuf,
     December 15, 1753.